graduates ask me about the next steps in their careers, I will refer them to The Essential Job Interview Handbook as a solid resource to help them reflect on their experience and frame their answers."

—Thomas P. Chester, senior HR manager, Office of Human Resources,
Princeton University

THE ESSENTIAL JOB INTERVIEW HANDBOOK

A QUICK AND HANDY RESOURCE FOR EVERY JOB SEEKER

JEAN BAUR

CAREER
PRESS
Pompton Plains, NJ

THE ESSENTIAL JOB INTERVIEW HANDBOOK
Printed in the U.S.A.

To order this title, please call toll-free 1-800-CAREER-1 (NJ and Canada: 201-848-0310) to order using VISA or MasterCard, or for further information on books from Career Press.

The Career Press, Inc.
220 West Parkway, Unit 12
Pompton Plains, NJ 07444
www.careerpress.com

Library of Congress Cataloging-in-Publication Data

CIP Data Available Upon Request.

For my husband, Robert.

ACKNOWLEDGMENTS

Thank you to Orville Pierson for introducing me to Career Press, to Mary Glynn and Frank Harvey for reading a draft of the book, and to the talented team at Career Press. And to all the others who helped: You're the best!

CONTENTS

INTRODUCTION

A huge challenge in the interview process is preparing for the unknown. Even with a fairly detailed job description or a briefing by a knowledgeable recruiter, job candidates often don't know the company's needs or what will happen during the interview. Huge shifts take place that we—the ones being interviewed—can't predict. That is one of the reasons why interviewing successfully is so difficult; we have to pay close attention to what we're told and what we're not told, as well as to the many non-verbal signals we receive. And many people conducting the interview aren't well prepared, haven't been trained in interviewing, and often don't like the process.

The Essential Job Interview Handbook takes a practical approach to this critical challenge, and will help you prepare effectively for interviews; become familiar with different types of interview questions and answers that focus on a wide range of functions including science, IT, finance, and marketing; know what to do after an interview; and then put it all together. You will learn how to integrate the intangibles with solid practice. What's unique about this approach is that it's both proprietary and road-tested. These are strategies that I've developed throughout my 19 years as a career coach and I've seen firsthand that they work.

The body of the book consists of sample questions with answers—multiple answers with an evaluation of what makes the best one. By going through these common interview questions, you are not only given an immediate way to do better on interviews, but you will also gain an understanding of successful strategies. In other words, instead of a list of questions with possible answers, this book puts those samples into a context that will prepare you for any situation.

Other interview books don't:

✓ use the MAP that is a critical part of both preparation and doing well in all-day interviews.
✓ give you a systematic way to probe for needs.
✓ explain what makes the best answer.
✓ base the interview questions and answers on years of coaching job seekers of all functions and levels.
✓ provide a critical technique for turning negative or difficult questions around.
✓ help you find a way to subtly "run" the interview or support an interviewer who is unprepared, inexperienced, or distracted.

This book has five sections: Preparation, Types of Questions, Types of Interviews, Managing Expectations, and Putting It All Together. In each chapter there is an overview that proposes major concepts, followed by case studies, work sheets, sample questions and answers, and useful templates. Next, you'll find a fun section called Ditch It!, which are examples of weak responses to interview questions that you want to avoid, accompanied by a brief explanation of why they're ineffective. The last section is Tips, a list that distills the major points of the chapter and that adds additional information.

What makes this book different from many on the market is how it teaches readers to think strategically. Let's say I'm asked a typical interview question such as: "Jean, why have you pursued jobs in so many different fields?"

1. My first task is to figure out the essence of what the interviewer is after. Are they worried I'm not going to be committed to the job? Or are they simply curious about how I managed to make several career changes?

2. Next I'm going to focus on the job I'm interviewing for and what I know so far about both the person interviewing me and the company. Let's say it's an outplacement firm looking for a career coach and I'm meeting with the person who would be my boss.

3. Now I bring these two pieces, the job description and what I know about their needs, together. In other words, I've recognized the type of question this is (preliminary or substance) and have taken a few seconds to figure how to use my answer to make a key selling point.

4. My answer: "I've been lucky to have had a wide and diverse experience as a writer, corporate trainer, and career coach. What I've discovered is that, rather than being three separate areas of expertise, these all boil down to communications. So, for example, in my extensive work as a career coach over the past 19 years, I use my writing and training skills to help clients communicate effectively, which is critical in networking and in making sure they ace their interviews."

5. Debrief: If I were interviewing for a writing position or one in training, then my example would be drawn from those areas, not my career coaching work. I think of this as a funnel: Broad concepts need to be brought down to specifics. Another way to look at this is headline and example: give an overview that paints the big picture and then prove it through an accomplishment story. (See Chapter 2 for more on

this subject.) Right now this process can feel like way too much work and you might be wondering how you could possibly go through these steps without waiting five minutes to answer the question. The quick answer is practice. With practice this becomes much easier. Think of interviewing well as developing new muscles. You can't do that in a day, but with regular exercise you'll get stronger and more agile a little at a time. Just be willing to start and I promise you this becomes second nature.

In looking for work, it's easy to get lost and discouraged. Although no book has all the answers to a complicated and unpredictable process (that many people dislike intensely), my hope is that *The Essential Job Interview Handbook* will give you an excellent foundation for this critical part of finding your next job, and very good company for the journey. The people whose stories you'll learn about in this book are real. They've been through a wide range of interview experiences as they looked for their next position, and some examples illustrate how tough it can be. But they kept going, they learned from the process, and persevered. They didn't let the down parts of the ups and downs, stop them. And they made it to another opportunity even if this ended up being different from their initial goals.

A note on confidentiality: None of the examples in this book are based on a single client. I've stuck to things that really happened, but drew from several resources both to make a point and to protect my clients' anonymity. In the outplacement field, as in other kinds of counseling, confidentiality is critical.

I am deeply grateful for my 16-plus years with Lee Hecht Harrison, a leading talent solutions company, and for all of the wonderful job seekers I've had the privilege to work with. You are my teachers and I'm always amazed by your courage as you enter the job search arena and prove to others how talented and valuable you are.

PART I

PREPARATION

1

WHERE TO START?

It's the moment all job seekers are waiting for: you receive a call and schedule an interview. There is a surge of hope as you think about working again and how exciting it could be to join this company. In addition, you dream of the huge relief that your search is over.

However, the excitement is quickly mixed with panic. What should you do? How will you get ready? And most importantly, how can you know what they really want?

Let's back up for a minute to see what you already know:

- ✓ The name of the company.
- ✓ How they found you.
- ✓ The industry.
- ✓ The title (and hopefully a job description).
- ✓ The date, time, and place of the interview.
- ✓ How many people you're seeing (and eventually a schedule that includes their names and titles) or if it's simply a screening interview.

   ✓ Contact information for the person who set this up (often a recruiter, agency, or HR representative).

As a friend of mine likes to say, "Facts are friendly," meaning I think that solid information is helpful and is the best place to start. So if you know the name of the company (and there are times when recruiters don't give this to you up front), you can begin your research. You could start with the company's website, but be careful not to stop there, as there may be more useful information on other websites or in industry journals and blogs.

You must know what the company does and be up-to-date with their current situation. If they've just acquired a small biotech company, you need to know about it as it could affect your potential job at the company. Having this up-to-date research at your fingertips is one of the most effective ways to prove you're interested in the company. Never wing it and ask, "What does your company do?" That's the quick path to a polite, "Thank you for coming in" and the interview is over.

If research isn't your thing and you're struggling to find good information on the company, go to your local public library and ask the reference librarian for help. They're skilled at finding even obsolete information.

Now that you've done some research, think about how the company found you, or in some cases, how you found them. If it was through an Internet ad, study the job description, but keep in mind that those descriptions are almost always incomplete and in some cases inaccurate. If you were referred in by a networking contact, ask that person for a convenient time to find out what they know about the company. In some cases they may have inside information, such as why the position is open or how the department is structured, which could be very useful to you. Most recruiters have solid working relationships with the companies they submit candidates to, so make sure to ask, if you're using a recruiter, what they know about the company, the people you'll be meeting, and any other general information. It's in their interest for you to do well. And lastly, if you targeted the company directly by emailing the hiring manager, review what you put in that email.

Next, make sure you're up-to-date in the industry. Let's say you're going to interview with Campbell's Soup. You need to know what their new products are, who their competition is, how their business is doing, and new trends or challenges that affect not only Campbell's, but other companies in the food industry. There are industry journals, blogs, and associations that can help you find this critical information.

Now take a careful look at the title and job description. Titles can vary wildly from one company to another, so it's best to study the scope of the job itself without getting concerned about the title. From what you know so far, ask yourself: "What is the most important thing the person in the position must do?" Start thinking about how your particular background fits or meets this need. In the sidebar there's an interview MAP that is going to help you specifically structure how your qualifications meet their requirements. Your interview MAP will help you stay on track, reduce nervousness, and document the main points you've covered with each interviewer.

If you're seeing three people, create a MAP for each meeting with the name of the company and the name and title of the person at the top. In the left column put the job description and what you've learned from your research. In the right, list key words to remind you of your qualifications and accomplishments that match the company's qualifications. If, for example, they want someone with three to five years' experience, that would be listed in the left column, and if you have six years of experience, you put that in the right column. I know you may be thinking, "How silly is that? There's no way I'd ever forget how long I've worked!" However, in my experience of coaching thousands of job seekers, it's amazing what can happen under stress. So even if you never refer to your MAP during an interview, I believe you'll find it helpful. Just knowing that it's there in your portfolio is a comfort, and if you hit a nervous moment or two, you can open your portfolio, glance down at your notes, and regain your confidence.

Also take note of the date, time, and location of the interview. Check the directions carefully; many career coaches recommend taking a dry run if it is reasonable. If you have to fly to a distant location, make sure you have all the travel information as well as someone to contact if there's a problem. And if you have to purchase the tickets yourself, ask how you'll be reimbursed. If a recruiter is involved, they should handle these logistics.

Try to give yourself unstructured time both the day before and the day after the interview. This is an exhausting process and you want to give yourself every possible advantage. Scheduling three interviews in one week is rarely a good idea. As soon as you can, get a sense of how the interview is expected to run. Will it be a panel with eight people asking you questions at once? If you're a scientist, when will your presentation be given and how many people will be attending? Is it one of those all-day affairs where you might be put in a conference room and the interviewers come in one after the other? We'll talk later about how to survive these "meat-grinder" interviews. Ask for the schedule and the names and titles of the people who will be seeing you. This allows you to learn something about them (through LinkedIn, Google, and so on) and it gives you time to practice pronouncing difficult names. Many times candidates are told "We'll give you the schedule when you arrive." Ask firmly but politely to have it now if possible.

The Interview Map

XYZ, Inc

Interview with Cathy Jones, MD and CEO for Director of Operations/Medical Affairs position, 1/8/13

KEY COMPONENTS OF POSITION	MATCHING ACCOMPLISHMENTS
Design operational processes to allow efficient execution of high-quality clinical studies, as per regulations	*Established and refined SOPs for IIT program, Training, Clinical Trial Disclosure, Contracting, Clinical system management*
Ensure consistency of operational approach across studies and development programs	*Do through training, work toward one system, team collaboration, communication top down, incorporate into IDPs*
Supervise implementation of clinical studies in compliance with Regs and SOPs	*Med Dev—add stats*
Prepare medical affairs related reports, such as postmarketing clinical study reports, and annual reports, etc.	*Clinical trial disclosure on CT.gov, annual IND, safety reporting requirements (should be coordinator with regulatory, safety, clinical research). Managed clinical trial coordination, worked with drug safety for quarterly or annual safety reports*

Manage compliance issues and develop cost estimates/budgets for postmarketing trials	*Have budget templates, work as a team on requirements. Used Grants Manager system to provide initial budget guidance*
Leadership ability to motivate	*I thrive in fast-paced, ambiguous, changing environments. I am a problem-solver, organizer, leader, and implementer*
Project management; resource allocation & fiscal management	*I have managed 3 to 4 diverse support groups while being responsible for 4 to 5 projects/initiatives*
Contract negotiation and management of vendor relationships	*Negotiated site contracts and part of negotiations for IVRS vendor, consultants, and system deployment vendor*
Understand complex clinical compliance issues; FDA regulations, GCP, ICH, global regulations and requirements	*Established unique distribution control and free drug programs for regulated drug, implemented CTMS*

Your questions for them:

1. What do you see as the biggest challenges for the person in this role?

2. How would a person in this position know how they are doing? Performance management system/feedback?

3. How much of the work is outsourced?

4. What percent of people in the Newark office will be new hires (not transitioning from Dallas)?

5. What impresses you most about your company?

Ditch It

1. *What does your company do?* This is insulting to the company as it shows you haven't even visited their website.

2. *Sure, I can come in for an interview this afternoon.* Two problems here: It communicates that you're not busy and it doesn't allow you enough time to prepare properly for the interview.

3. *I've got to take the kids to the dentist so I can't come in.* Of course you have other commitments, but don't be specific about what they are. Instead, say, "I have a conflict that afternoon, but can change it if that's the best time for you."

Tips

✓ Research the company carefully and don't rely solely on their website.

✓ If possible, give yourself enough time before the interview so that you're well prepared and rested.

✓ Ask for a list of who you'll be seeing, including their titles.

✓ Make sure you have the name and number of a contact person as well as good directions.

✓ Prepare your interview MAP (one copy for each person you'll see) and include your questions for the interviewers at the bottom.

✓ See if anyone in your network works for or has worked for the company and ask them for additional information.

✓ Knowing about the company and the people you'll be meeting with gives you a huge edge. This information

will help you select the most appropriate accomplishment examples (to prove you're the right one for
the job), and is one of the best ways to demonstrate
interest in the company. You can't say you'd love to
join them if you aren't up-to-date on their latest
initiatives.

2

GET YOUR STORIES STRAIGHT!

How can you come up with a strategy or know how to prepare for an interview when you don't know what will happen? If you think of having a plan for the interview as part of your preparation, and understand that many aspects of the interview may change, then you have positioned yourself in the best possible way.

You've done your research and now have an interview MAP for each person you're seeing unless it's a panel interview. An important part of your MAP is creating accomplishment examples or stories that prove your credentials. In other words, you have to learn how to talk effectively about yourself. We'll look at how to do this after exploring a few strategy examples.

A Convention/Meeting Planner has an interview and matches most of the company's job description. She has planned large meetings, negotiated with vendors, managed complex budgets, and dealt with all of the logistics of bringing many people to one place. One of their requirements is international experience, but she doesn't have this. What can she do to prepare for questions on this topic?

- ✓ Talk to other Convention Planners who do have international experience and find out what the particular issues or needs are.
- ✓ Look at published information from her professional association or journals to see if there are resources for international events.
- ✓ See if there is any way she could volunteer with an organization that is hosting an international event near where she lives.
- ✓ Research this specific topic.
- ✓ Come up with an accomplishment story or example that proves her ability to learn new skills or functions quickly and effectively.

The goal of a Senior Finance Manager with a strong background in manufacturing, is to become CFO (Chief Financial Officer). He has never held this title, but with 20 years of experience and a strong network that keeps him up-to-date in his field, he believes he has the qualifications for the job. Through his network he is referred to the CEO of a small manufacturing company and has an interview scheduled. How can he prepare for the most critical question: "Why should we hire you as CFO when you've never held that position?"

- ✓ Outline the scope of his responsibilities and, in his MAP, prove that although he hasn't held the CFO title, he has already successfully managed many of the requirements.
- ✓ Research the challenges facing this company and create a 30-60-90-day plan. This will give the CEO concrete examples of what this candidate would do if he is hired.
- ✓ Create a list of questions that again prove his value to the company and illustrate that he is a big-picture thinker.
- ✓ Take the contact who referred him to the company out for lunch and ask for advice. This is the person

who saw him as a good match, so his or her help will be invaluable.

On the right side of your MAP, where you have a brief reminder of the story or example you want to use to prove how well you match what the company is looking for, you need to prepare in detail exactly what the situation was, what you did, and the end results. This is similar to the accomplishment statements or bullets on your resume, except that in this case you'll be talking and can go into much more detail. (And in interviews you also must expect to be interrupted as you talk, because the interviewer may want more details about a particular area.)

There are several acronyms for this structure, but my favorite is PAR, which stands for **P**roblem, **A**ction, and **R**esult, because it's simple, easy to remember, and gets to the point. PAR is your scaffolding; it will support your answers and make it easy for the interviewer(s) to follow you. And most importantly, it will keep you from rambling. Follow this template for the bulk of your answers and you will do very well. Let's look at a few examples of accomplishment stories to see what makes them effective:

Career Coach

Developed and delivered two ancillary outplacement workshops: "Polishing Your Interview Image" and "Organizing Your Job Search" to help clients improve their confidence and efficiency in the search process.

Problem: People in transition often need help with how they look and how they go about looking for work.

Action: "Developed and delivered" tells us that this person is creative, proactive, and is also a trainer.

Results: This can't be quantified, but still it's important to note that for this career coach, there is a strong, two-part benefit to the clients.

Note: This was from the resume of a friend of mine, and she left out the last part of the bullet (the part about improving confidence and efficiency) until I told her to do it. To her, it was obvious—she knew the value of these two workshops she had designed and given—but the interviewer didn't. As you're creating your list of accomplishment stories that are a critical part of your interview preparation, ask yourself: So what? I know this sounds a bit rude, but in my work with thousands of people in transition, it really helps in getting to the selling point or results.

IT Professional

Recruited by a Director of Information Technology to develop a Data Warehouse and Business Intelligence infrastructure to support Residential Mortgage Financial Reporting, Master Servicing, and Analytic Team.

Problem: This bullet starts with an action that implies the problem: The company didn't have the infrastructure they needed to handle technology efficiently.

Action: "Develop" and "support" tells us the key roles this person played.

Results: We know the three areas in the company that are now improved: Residential Mortgage Financial Reporting, Master Servicing, and the Analytical Team.

Scientist

Designed new synthesis routes, developed new reaction conditions, and modified reaction procedures to optimize the yield, processes, safety, and efficiency. Published patents and papers on the new processes.

Problem: A scientist would get this better than I would, but it looks as if a lab procedure needed improvement.

Action: This person "designed, developed, and modified."

Result: He improved "yield, processes, safety, and efficiency"—quite a complex accomplishment—and by adding publishing and patents, gives outside credibility to the worth of this work.

Ditch It

1. *Isn't it obvious I can do the job?* Never assume that someone "gets" your fit without proof. Build a list of strong accomplishment examples so that you can offer verification that you can do the job.

2. *I don't need to know who I'm seeing until I come in for the interview.* Why would you create this kind of pressure for yourself? The more you know ahead of time, the better you'll do.

3. *As you can see from my resume.* It would be wonderful if you could count on interviewers having read your resume, but you can't. Don't use this phrase, but rather be prepared to explain your background in detail.

Tips

- ✓ Have a MAP or plan, but realize that it would be unusual for the interview to follow it.
- ✓ Select the accomplishments from your background that best meet the job requirements as you know them.
- ✓ Devise a strategy for talking about gaps or parts of your background that may be missing from what the company requires (for example, no college degree, lack of a certification, and no international experience).
- ✓ Get help from others if you're new to the industry or lack other key information.

✓ As you review the right side of your MAP where you've listed your accomplishments, ask yourself, "So what?" to make sure you highlight results.

3

FIGURE OUT WHAT EMPLOYERS WANT

Figuring out what employers want might seem like an odd idea if you have a detailed job description or are working with a recruiter who has filled you in on the position, company culture, and the people you'll be meeting. And because you've already researched the company carefully and spoken to inside contacts if you can find them (LinkedIn is really helpful), it's understandable that many people getting ready to go on interviews think that this is enough. Unfortunately, it isn't because of the following reasons:

- ✓ The job description is out-of-date.
- ✓ The job description wasn't written by the hiring manager and therefore may not reflect his or her most important needs.
- ✓ Someone was just promoted or retired so the department needs to reorganize.
- ✓ A new project or contract has changed the top priorities.
- ✓ The company has recently gone through a downsizing or an acquisition so roles are being realigned.

The basic issue here is not to make assumptions—don't assume you know exactly what they're looking for. So part of your preparation is to plan the questions you will ask them. On the interview MAP that we looked at in Chapter 1, you'll see a number of questions written at the bottom. A critical part of your interview preparation is coming up with questions that will highlight your strengths, illustrate your professionalism, and ensure that you've hit the bull's-eye of their most important needs.

This is where the ZAP technique comes in—a wonderful tool developed by the training firm, Communispond's outplacement division in the 1980s. ZAP stands for: **Z**ero in on the most critical needs, **A**sk questions, and **P**rovide an answer with a selling point (this is what proves you can do the job).

Let's see how this process works in action. I'm at an interview and the job description is not well defined and HR or the hiring manager (by this I mean the person who would be my boss) asks me the common preliminary question: "Jean, tell me about yourself."

I could start my answer with a broad statement that gives the headline of my background, such as: "I'm a career counselor and author with many years experience in the outplacement industry, and I've also worked extensively as a trainer, executive coach, and writer."

But rather than continuing at this point, it could be really smart to ZAP so that I know which part of my background is of interest to them. If I go on and on about the business writing and presentation skills courses I not only helped develop but also delivered, they may be disinterested and tune out. The question or ZAP that I might use would be: "Is there a particular area you'd like me to concentrate on? The job description seems like a good fit, but I want to make sure I understand your needs."

You might decide that you only need the first part of ZAP and that would be fine. What I do then is give a brief response to a question and then ask for clarification or more information.

But what if I'm asked a question and really don't have a clue as to how to answer? In that case, I could ZAP first. Let's look at how I might do it for the same tell-me-about-yourself question: "I'd be glad to tell you about myself, but would you mind giving me a little more detail about this job? I want to make sure I include relevant parts of my background."

And if you want to be superpolite, you can start this initial ZAP by asking: "Could I ask you a question first? Would that be all right?"

Your goal is the same whether you ZAP after you give an answer or before, and that is to make sure you know what the company or individual wants. This is the target that all your answers must address.

There is an added benefit to using ZAP: An interviewer who is inexperienced or uncomfortable may dread having to carry the responsibility of keeping the conversation going. By asking questions, you're taking some of that burden off of them. But keep in mind, styles differ and there are interviewers who don't want you to ask questions. Pay attention, try it at the appropriate moment (often about halfway into the interview process), and never try to take total control of the interview. As I tell my clients: "You're the guest. Let them take the lead."

What's for Dinner?

More than 10 years ago I designed an interview class for Lee Hecht Harrison called "Interview Techniques That Could Save Your Life." As I teach my clients how to ZAP, we talk about ways to practice this effective probing technique. I ask them how they might respond using ZAP to a simple question from someone they live with: "What's for dinner?"

Here are some sample responses:

✓ Dinner?
✓ You're cooking?
✓ Are you taking me out?

We always have a good laugh over this one, but it's a good illustration of how creative this question-question is. Most of us are wired to instantly answer what we're asked, but with ZAP, you have a strategy that gives you a little buffer between the question and your answer, and often the response to your question gives you additional information so that your answer is stronger.

Going back to an issue we looked at in Chapter 2, how could ZAP have helped the event planner who doesn't have international experience? The question she dreaded, was: "Why should we hire you when you haven't had international experience?" So to get out of this tight spot where all she can think of saying is, "I don't know" or, "Because I'm really good at event planning," she could ZAP:

- ✓ "Could I ask you what your primary concerns are regarding international events?"
- ✓ "Are you concerned about cultural issues or the logistics of setting up events in other countries?"

In other words, by asking these questions, she's honing in on what is on that interviewer's mind, and hopefully his or her answer gives her a foothold for a decent answer. Of course you never lie, but the ZAP technique gives you a strategic tool to position yourself as effectively as possible. Lastly, keep in mind that few candidates match every requirement. If you show intelligence and enthusiasm (and asking questions is one great way to do this), you may get hired over a more qualified candidate.

Ditch It

1. *Why is there so much turnover in your company?* This could be an important question to ask, but the way you ask it is critical. The danger with this question is that it is negative and could embarrass the interviewer. If this is an issue that you've uncovered in your

research, you might want to turn it around to sound like: "What kinds of things is your company doing to retain productive employees?" Notice you've given the interviewer an easy out by using the word *productive*.

2. *Why did you get beat out by the competition?* There could be situations where you could use this question safely, but in many cases it's too negative and could make the interviewer feel uncomfortable. It's critical, however, that you know about the competition, but that you ask about it in more subtle ways.

3. *Did the person who held this position previously get fired?* This is none of your business and therefore it comes across as a rude question. If you wanted to soften it you could ask: "May I ask why this position is open?" Notice that you've asked permission—a great way to take the edge off a question.

Tips

- ✓ A critical part of your interview preparation is deciding which questions you may need to ask to make sure you're addressing the company's needs.
- ✓ Don't wait for an interview to practice learning how to ZAP. In your daily conversations, see what happens if you ask a question before you answer a question.
- ✓ Pay attention to the interviewer's style so that you can see if he or she is open to questions.
- ✓ Never lie but use the ZAP technique to position yourself strategically.
- ✓ When used successfully, using ZAP makes the interview more of a conversation and less of an interrogation. This is a much better way for people to share information, but again, be sensitive to different styles of interviewing.

4

REPHRASE AND REFRAME

Right now, you might now be thinking: "What else could I possibly need to do? Isn't all this preparation a bit much?" You may also remember that you didn't have to do all this work to get your last job. But because interviews are difficult to get in general, and in a tough economy like our current one, you're also facing intense competition, you can't assume it will be easy to get an offer.

As part of your preparation, you want to think about what you can do when you're asked a negative or difficult question. Later in the chapter, we'll look at some extreme examples of these, and as I tell my clients in my interview class, if you can survive these questions, you won't have any difficulty with the others. Interviewers sometimes take a confrontational tone to test candidates to see how they react to stress. The huge challenge here is that if you simply answer a hostile question without creating a buffer first, you're likely to come across as defensive and weak. For example: "How can you say you have good organizational skills when that critical project you just mentioned failed?"

Your answer could be something like: "I worked really hard on it, but I had to deal with other departments and they didn't make their deadlines, so the failure was really out of my hands."

This is not a great answer because:

✓ You blame others for the project failure.
✓ You repeat the word *failure,* making a bad situation worse.
✓ You take no responsibility for what happened.
✓ It sounds as if your ability to communicate with, and motivate others, is weak.
✓ No one cares if you worked hard if you weren't effective

When faced with a tough question, you should rephrase it and then answer it. "Is the project I mentioned a fair example of my organizational skills?" or "How are my organizational skills and the project I mentioned related?" or "What factors led to project results that didn't meet our expectations?" Keep in mind that these are rhetorical questions (ones you ask aloud but are not expecting the interviewer to answer). Let's break this down step-by-step. When faced with a negative or difficult question, you need to:

✓ Listen for the concept of the question (that is what this is really about?).
✓ Think of neutral or positive words to replace the negative ones (the word *failed*, for example, could be replaced by "didn't meet expectations").
✓ See if there is faulty logic that needs to be replaced (in this case the questioner has linked organizational skills to the project's failure, which might not be related).
✓ Create a rhetorical question (this means one you say aloud without expecting an answer), say it aloud, and then answer the question. Rephrases often start with: what, when, how, who, and why.

So here's the sequence again, using the same question:

Interviewer: "How can you say you have good organizational skills when that critical project you just mentioned failed?"

You: "What factors led to project results that didn't meet our expectations? When we set up the timeline for this project, we were using a local vendor, and if there hadn't been changes, we would have succeeded. But as part of a cost-saving initiative, we had to outsource that work. Because we were unfamiliar with the organization that was now providing our supplies, we were unable to anticipate the lag between orders and delivery. Once I realized what had happened, I revised our contract with them so that if the deliverables didn't meet our deadlines, they paid a penalty. This quickly resolved the problem."

What just happened? The person being interviewed took a negative question and by first rephrasing it, used it to illustrate how effective she was in fixing a problem. Notice that she didn't need to talk about organizational skills because the details of her answer showed them in action. Nothing beats concrete examples. Specifics, not generalizations are your most effective sales tools.

Now you may be thinking: *Who has time to go through all these steps before answering a question?* If you have an interview in the next week or two, my advice would be to forget all about it. But if you have time, if you can practice and build the rephrase skill into your overall communications, then you have a wonderful tool for dealing with negative or difficult questions. So like the ZAP technique, you can practice rephrasing in your everyday conversations. Here are a few examples:

"Why can't we go to Disney World for our vacation this year?"

Rephrase: "What are our vacation plans?" or "Where are we thinking of going on vacation this year?" or "What kind of vacation makes sense while I'm in transition?" (Notice I never use the phrase "out of work" or "unemployed." It is way too negative.)

"Why did you buy a new suit when you're out of work?"

Rephrase: "Was it a good idea to make an investment in my appearance during a job search?"

"How do you know you'll find a job before we run out of money?"

Rephrase: "What backup plans do I have if my search takes longer than expected?"

Notice how much work the rephrasing does. In many cases, they almost make the eventual answer unnecessary. Another thing you might notice is what I like to call the "Tai Chi of rephrase." Instead of getting into a fistfight with the interviewer or your spouse or child, you're sidestepping confrontation while still addressing the real issue. This is the power of rephrasing: It makes you look good, doesn't escalate negative questions, and keeps you from sounding defensive or weak.

Evil Questions

It's highly unlike that you'll ever be asked questions as mean as these, but I use them in my interview class simply to illustrate the power of the rephrase technique. As I mentioned earlier, if you can rephrase these, you can rephrase anything.

If you're so smart, why did your previous company let you go?

What circumstances led XYZ company to downsize its entire research lab?

Aren't you just interested in this job for the money?

What it is about joining a leader in the food industry that I find particularly exciting?

Aren't you getting ready to retire?

What are my career goals?

Why have you worked for so many companies?

How did I get such a diverse background?

Isn't it true that you have a history of making enemies at work?

How do I get along with my coworkers? or *What would my references say about my relationships at work?*

Aren't you out of date in your field?

How current am I in organizational development?

Do you want to telecommute so that you can take care of your children?

What advantages does a flexible schedule have for both me and your company?

Didn't your former company pay you more than you're worth?

How did XYZ determine my compensation?

How well do you take criticism?

How has feedback made me a better manager?

Why are you still in the job market?

What criteria are important in my search that may affect how long it takes me to find the right position?

Ditch It

1. *Why would you ask me such a thing?* You've been hit with a negative question and are now making it worse by confronting the interviewer.

2. *I'm divorced and have custody of my three children so of course I can't work late.* As teenagers so succinctly put

it, TMI—too much information! It's reasonable to find out about the workday and the company's expectations, but you don't have to give reasons why your day needs to end at 5 p.m. And if you do need to say something about why you need to leave on time, you might do better to say that you have other obligations.

3. *Talk to my references. They'll tell you I'm a hard worker.* Using your references as part of an answer isn't a bad idea, but it's your job, not theirs, to prove that you work hard. Use a specific accomplishment or PAR story (Chapter 2) so that the interviewer comes to the conclusion that you're a great worker. Flat statements about how wonderful we are rarely work.

Tips

- ✓ Train yourself so that you don't always automatically answer questions.
- ✓ Listen for the concept of a difficult or negative question and find neutral or positive language to use in your rephrase.
- ✓ Don't stray from the concept or you'll make a bad situation worse. The interviewer is likely to get annoyed and say, "That's not what I asked you!"
- ✓ Practice rephrasing in your daily life. The grocery clerk says, "Paper or plastic." And you say: "What kind of bag would I like?" This will make it easier for you to rephrase when you need to.
- ✓ Keep in mind that rephrasing or reframing are part of excellent listening skills. You're not doing what many politicians do, which is to give a rote answer from their platform that doesn't answer the question. Instead, you are using a powerful strategy to turn a challenge to your advantage while accurately answering the question.

5

FINAL PREPARATION: FIRST IMPRESSIONS

When teaching classes on interviewing, I often start by asking how long we have to make a first impression. Most experts agree it's in the three-second range. How we look (grooming, clothing, jewelry, posture, gesture, facial expressions, and handshake), and how we sound (volume, inflection, pace, and accents) contribute to this lightening fast snapshot.

And because some of these issues take time to address, it's a ⟨…⟩u are coming across as part of your ⟨…⟩go down this list and see what you

⟨…⟩in this category is everything that would ⟨…⟩appearance. This would mean that your fin-⟨…⟩trimmed (for men) or nicely manicured (for ⟨…⟩oes for your hair. Makeup on women should ⟨…⟩points and minimize imperfections. Profes-⟨…⟩sn't draw attention to itself, but creates the im-⟨…⟩nter you.

Clothing. It's amazing what clothing can do for us. For women, I think it's common to feel that we've "worn the wrong thing to work." Our clothing styles can be very diverse, so get advice from someone with a good sense of style about what you plan to wear to an interview. Also, make sure to have more than one outfit, as you may get asked to come back in a few days for a second interview and you don't want to wear the same outfit. (Men can get away with this by wearing a different shirt and tie with the same suit.)

Match your clothing to your industry. If you're in banking, wear a navy blue, gray, or black suit (pantsuits are fine for women). But if you're in marketing, training, or academia, you have a wider choice. I like to wear bright colors such as a red or turquoise, as they complement my coloring and reflect my personal style.

Jewelry. At my first interview in the outplacement industry, one of the VPs (a man) asked me what I thought about men wearing jewelry. Without looking carefully at him, I replied: "I think a ring and a watch are fine, but beyond that I wouldn't recommend it." Then I looked up and saw that he was wearing several rings and a big gold bracelet. I blushed, we moved on to other issues, and I still got the job. Keep your jewelry subtle unless you're an opera singer or nightclub entertainer. And don't wear things that will clank when you rest your hand on the table or that make noise when you gesture. I have a charm bracelet that I've had since seventh grade that I love, but I don't wear it to interviews.

Posture. You don't have to look as if you're serving in the Marines, but a good, straight posture conveys confidence and attention. Because I had to demonstrate good posture in my years teaching presentation skills, I trained myself to rarely sit back in a chair. I sit on the front half with both feet on the floor, my back straight, and my shoulders back. What does this say? *I'm here, I'm interested, I'm full of energy.* I firmly believe that if you're going to have good posture at an interview, you must cultivate it as a daily habit. Also, don't cross your legs or let your legs bounce up and down. These bad habits distract the interviewer and undercut your strong message about your capabilities.

Gesture. If you talk with your hands you've probably been told to keep them still. That's not what I would recommend. Gestures need to convey meaning, because they bring your message alive. So if you're explaining that you managed a huge project, that key word *huge* demands a gesture. The way you gesture will be your own, but work on developing "gesture awareness." In other words, what phrases will really come alive if your hands add motion, description, or emphasis?

Let's say you're talking about "channeling resources." You want to paint a picture of that keyword *channeling*, so your hands could start palms facing each other at about body width, and then you'd move them forward as you bring them closer together. That will help the interviewer see and feel this key point. Try in your everyday conversations to build gesture awareness and let your hands be descriptive. Lastly, find a neutral way to rest them, either on the table or desk if there is one, or on your lap or on the arms of your chair. But don't lace your fingers together and play with your rings, as these are unproductive ways to release energy.

Facial expression. Referring back to that lightning-fast snapshot we take when we first meet people, much of that impression will be created by our facial expressions. If we're frowning or our faces look frozen in nervousness, the interviewer could easily get the impression that we're difficult or indifferent. But if we smile, looking him or her in the eyes, then we create a strong, positive impression and are helping to get the interview off on the right foot. We'll talk a bit later about getting specific feedback on how we look (and the importance of eye contact), but for now, be aware of what your face is communicating.

Handshake. This is an easy one: Avoid the extremes. No one likes to have their knuckles crushed and the weak "dead fish" handshake is a huge turnoff. Grasp the interviewer's hand firmly, letting your hand fully engage with theirs. (The fingertip handshake is almost as bad as the dead fish one.) As you give your initial greeting (often something like, "Very nice to meet you") look the interviewer in the eye and smile. A smile that only moves your mouth is often a cold one; make sure you're smiling with your eyes as well. Because eyes are critical to first impressions, the sidebar will address eye contact in detail.

How we sound, or voice. Isn't it awful to hear your own voice recorded? When I leave a message on my phone and then listen to it, I always think that I can't sound like that! Volume is probably the easiest part of voice to address, so work on increasing your volume if you notice that the people you're talking with are always asking to repeat yourself. Being too loud also causes a problem, as it's often interpreted as aggression. When I'm talking on the phone and get excited, I subconsciously increase my volume, so I have to remind myself to speak more softly. Inflection is the changes in pitch that keeps us from talking in a monotone. Listen to really good speakers like Dr. Martin Luther King Jr. and you'll hear a wonderful use of inflection that adds interest and emphasis to his words. Pace is the speed at which we talk (and having lived in New York City a long time, my pace is still fast). In addition to being hard to understand, a fast pace can convey nervousness and/or impatience. And lastly, our accents—whether regional or from living in another country—paint part of the picture. I was recently on a customer service call and the woman helping me was from the south. She had a slow and deliberate way of talking, her southern accent drawing out the vowels in her words, that had a comforting effect on me. To see how deeply accents affect us, notice how many TV commercials use actors with British accents, because they convey authority.

"Eye" Got It!

Several years ago I was asked to coach a senior executive who wasn't in transition. I was hired because of my training and coaching background, and top management at this company had identified Sylvia as a scientist ready to make the leap to top management. But they had a problem: she didn't come across as senior manager material and one of the reasons was her poor eye contact.

At our initial meeting I outlined what I thought we should cover in our sessions together. We discussed her concerns and in the end agreed on a plan. The second time we met, we worked on an eye drill. On name tents I had drawn pairs of eyes and had placed them on top of the chairs around the conference table. This was her team. I used a video camera so that I could give her the chance to see herself—both before and after—I first taped her discussing a current project. I didn't coach her. Then, giving the same talk, I asked her to only talk when she had a pair of eyes in focus and asked her to stay with that pair of eyes for five full seconds—or about the time it takes to complete a thought. Every time her eyes flicked away, I reminded her to focus until I said "Okay," and she knew she could move on to the next "person." At first she claimed that she couldn't do it, that it was too unnatural. I asked her to hang in there, to stick with the exercise long enough to tape her delivering her talk only to eyes and then when she reviewed the tape, she could decide if this was a huge waste of time or not.

The before and after was startling. Sylvia saw how uncertain she looked when her eyes darted around the room, and how confident she appeared when her eye contact settled down. In the weeks ahead we worked on other presentation skills including posture, gesture, and voice, and I always coached her on her eye contact so that it became second nature. By talking to people, Sylvia came across as confident and concerned about her team and this helped her look the part of her new, senior management role.

Ditch It!

1.   *Leg jiggling—often done when your legs are crossed, but some people do this with both feet on the floor.* This highly

annoying behavior can undo the most wonderful verbal statements. It's distracting and would make most interviewers wonder if you're hyperactive, not telling the truth, or perhaps had too much coffee!

2. *Darting eyes that avoid sustained eye contact with the interviewer(s).* You could be the most sincere person on the planet, but if your eyes jump around and scan the room, the interviewer will almost always come to the conclusion that you're lying or trying to hide something. You may think this is "unfair," but my advice would be to practice solid eye contact as Sylvia did, so that you can use this powerful nonverbal behavior to your advantage.

3. *Your hands clutch each other and don't let go during the entire interview.* We are all attracted to and convinced by sound and motion. If your hands do none of the work and don't help the interviewer see that "huge" project you worked on, you're missing out on one of the key ways to convince the interviewer, show enthusiasm, and retain his or her interest. A "talking head"—relying on your voice only—is not going to make you look like the person who really wants the job.

4. *You're slumped in your chair.* Posture is important, as it can either say "I'm excited to be here, I can do this job!" or it can tell the interviewer: "I'm really tired and just need a paycheck." Practice good posture in your day-to-day life and it will be easier to impress your interviewers with your enthusiasm.

Tips

✓ Ask for feedback so that you can test out the first impression you're making. Be specific and include clothing, hair, posture, gesture, voice, eye contact, and handshake.

✓ Build the habit of good posture. Whether at work or at home or having lunch with a friend, see if you can sit and stand with your back straight, your shoulders back, and your feet firmly on the floor (and break the habit of crossing your legs).

✓ In your everyday conversations, pay attention to your eye contact. Are your eyes staying with the person you're talking with for a complete thought? Can you be careful not to scan the room?

✓ Do a careful review of your wardrobe and pick out networking and interview clothes that make you look good. Make sure your shoes are shined and that everything is cleaned and well pressed. Like it or not, the way you dress is a powerful part of first impressions.

✓ Read *Talk Your Way to the Top: How to Address Any Audience Like Your Career Depends On It,* by Kevin Daley and his daughter, Laura Daley-Caravella. This is one of the best books I've ever read on how to become a powerful speaker. (Kevin was the founder and chairman of Communispond.)

PART II

TYPES OF QUESTIONS

6

ICE-BREAKER QUESTIONS

Often thought of as "chitchat," ice breaker questions allow both the interviewer and the job candidate to get used to each other. The content of this type of question is deceptively simple and rarely includes issues of substance, but they're important nonetheless, as they form part of that powerful first impression.

Sometimes these questions could be asked by the receptionist, or by someone else who isn't part of the formal interview process. Don't let this fool you—it's highly likely that everyone has a vote of some sort and will come to conclusions such as "He seemed really nice," or "I enjoyed talking with her." Your job is to show everyone just how wonderful you are. No exceptions!

If there are circumstances that make the start of an interview particularly stressful, don't let that stop you from answering these warm-up questions. A client of mine had an interview in Holland for a wonderful job that would require him to move there. After discussing it with his family, he decided that it was such a good advancement for him (in the work he'd be doing as well as his title and compensation) that he couldn't turn it down. However, his flight was due in Amsterdam at 9 a.m. and didn't arrive until 10:30 a.m. By the time he got his luggage and got through customs, he realized that he wasn't going to have time to go to his hotel before his first meeting. The company had arranged a car service for him, so he did his best to freshen up on the way. He certainly didn't feel at his best after a night spent flying and no time for a shower. He called the company to explain why he would be late and finally walked into their building at noon.

He was whisked into a conference room and asked about his flight. He replied that it had been fine, but that unfortunately it had been delayed. The interview then started with no stop for lunch. While he struggled through some tough questions, he felt himself getting angry with the way he was being treated. He was tired, hungry, unfocused, and wishing with each question that he hadn't agreed to this interview. What saved him was his interview MAP; there in front of him was the list of job requirements and how he matched them. He took notes, drank water, finally asked if was possible to get a sandwich, and made it through a really challenging day. When he got to his hotel room, he collapsed and slept for a few hours before going out to dinner with the top executives.

When he and I reviewed his experience a week later, he had found out that this company had made his schedule close to impossible on purpose. Of course they didn't make his plane late, but they had structured his day to see how he would react to stress—in particular to things he couldn't control. The good news is that they liked what they saw and he got an offer. In this example, there was only one ice-breaker question—a seemingly innocent question about his flight. As part of their ethical training, medical students are taught, "Primum non nocere" or "First, do no harm," which is good advice to follow with ice-breaker questions. My client showed poise and endurance and started the interview off to his best possible advantage despite stressful circumstances.

Let's look at some typical ice-breaker questions and how you might answer them. I use three symbols to describe answers that are good (+A), better (*A), and best (!A) and also include a brief analysis of each answer in italics.

Thanks, Bill, for coming in today. Did you have any trouble finding us?

+A. No, it was an easy ride. *Bill gives a positive answer, which is good, but doesn't talk long enough for the interviewer to get used to his voice and style.*

*A. No, none at all. Your directions were perfect and I found your office with no difficulty. *This is a bit better as it's both longer and more complimentary.*

!A. No, none at all. Thank you for having your assistant give me such excellent directions. I thought it might take about 45 minutes, but I made the trip in half an hour. *This is the best answer as it both compliments the interviewer and gives additional information about the time it took Bill to get to the office. Don't do this if it takes you a long time to get to an interview, but a short commute is often seen as a plus by both parties.*

Nice to meet you, Nancy. Have you been here before?

+A. No, this is my first time. *Not a bad answer, but again too short.*

*A. No, I haven't. I've lived in the area for years and have passed the building, but this is the first time I've been in the office. *A better answer, this one gives a bit of Nancy's history and lets the interviewer know that Nancy lives nearby and has noticed the building.*

!A. No, Steve, I haven't, although I've driven past it many times. It's really stunning inside—very light and welcoming. *This could be the best answer as it uses the interviewer's name and shows that Nancy is observant. She also compliments the look of the building, again helping to create a positive way to start the interview.*

Joe, I see that you went to Villanova. That's my school, too.

+A. Were you on the football team? *Joe takes a bit of risk here by bringing up a specific activity. If the answer is no, he hasn't used the ice-breaker question to build rapport.*

*A. Great school, isn't it? I majored in economics. What about you? *A bit better, Joe shares some personal information that may or may not be on his resume. The risk here is that the interviewer doesn't want to talk about his or her major and isn't ready to be asked a question.*

!A. I felt very lucky go to there. I had originally thought that I would attend Penn State, but after a few visits to Villanova, I realized that it was the perfect school for me—large yet not too large, with a diverse student body and really wonderful faculty. *This upbeat answer does some serious work of letting the interviewer know important things about Joe: how he made the decision to go to Villanova and what he liked about the school. And by avoiding a specific activity (football) or a specific major (economics), he creates a safer platform for starting the interview. Notice in the first two sample answers, it is Joe who is asking the questions. Not asking the interviewer a question this early in the process is usually a better way to go.*

Really cold today, isn't it?

+A. Can't stand it! I wonder if spring will ever come? *You don't have to love winter, but this is a strong statement to make to an ice-breaker question, and if the interviewer is an avid snowboarder, you've just shot yourself in the foot.*

*A. Yes, it is. The wind is what really goes right through you. *A much safer answer. The job seeker doesn't let on whether he or she loves or hates winter weather.*

!A. Yes, it is. We've been so lucky to have had a mild winter; this arctic wind is really a surprise. But I grew up in Minnesota, so it doesn't bother me. *Chatting about the weather is a safe place to start and this interviewee shows that he or she is comfortable with this, and also adds a bit of personal history—again helping to make a connection with the interviewer.*

But what if, after looking at these samples, you're saying to yourself, "That's just not me! I can't do it!" This is often true for those with highly technical backgrounds, such as scientists, IT professionals, or engineers. Is there a way to combine that deep knowledge with an ice-breaker? I think it's worth a try, as you still need a bridge or transition before the interview really begins. So what if you said something like, "I'm excited to see your _____ (and you mention a piece of high-tech equipment that they have)." Or "I'm impressed by the way you solved that xyz problem." And yes, this is getting into substance questions, but it still gives the interviewer the chance to get to know you a little in a more relaxed setting.

Another way to go would be to think of a few questions that are general enough to be ice-breakers. An example would be: "Have you always used that program to integrate your systems?" These kinds of questions show that you've done your homework and that you're really interested in the company. Not a bad way to begin.

Nice Dip!

Years ago there used to be a wonderful handout called "Tips for Shy Networkers." I haven't been able to track it down as it was from the 90s, but I found it very helpful when I was working with introverted clients who were at a loss about how to introduce themselves to others, work a room, or basically network. One of the ice-breakers on that handout, which was to be used at the hors d'oeuvre table at a networking event, was a pithy "Nice dip" statement. This always made me laugh.

And yes, it's an ice-breaker, and might do a fine job of getting a conversation going, but to my ear, it's funny. So what should you say if you're at a meeting, feeling shy, and don't know anyone? I like "Is this your first time here?" and even if you say it to the chairwoman or some other official of the organization, you can quickly add, "I'm a new member of XYZ and am looking forward to tonight's speaker."

What you say as an ice-breaker, whether at a networking event or an interview, probably isn't as important as the fact that you are engaged in conversation—and what your nonverbal language is saying. You're trying to get past the first, awkward moments and create a strong, positive image that is basically saying, "I'm happy to be here, I'm interested in you and your company, and I look forward to our conversation." If "Nice dip" is useful, go ahead and say it. More importantly, pay attention to the other person, follow his or her lead, and make it easy to exchange these introductory statements that pave the way for the interview to follow.

And a last reminder for introverts: On February 6, 2012, *Time Magazine* published a wonderful article by Bryan Walsh, "The Upside of Being an Introvert (And Why Extroverts Are Overrated)." As Walsh talks about the power of introverts, he makes a key point about how creative introverts often are. Because introverts usually enjoy time by themselves, they tap into a deeper creative process and frequently come up with excellent solutions. So if starting conversations is difficult for you, please remember the value that you bring to your work, and in your own style, find a way to engage in the back and forth that is the basis for effective interviewing.

Ditch It!

1. *I'm sick and tired of all this rain! I think it's time to build an ark.* Ice-breaker conversations about the weather are not the time to vent your frustrations with the rain or cold or whatever is bothering you. The interviewer

could quickly decide you have some anger issues and cut the interview short.

2. *I've got a GPS system so I never get lost.* That's good that you're using technology to get to the interview on time, but it's more gracious to either state that you had no problem finding the office, or to thank the person who sent you directions.

3. *Haven't we met somewhere before?* This could be an uncomfortable question to an interviewer, because it puts them on the spot and might distract them as they try to remember if they met you at a party or at their son's Boy Scout meeting.

Tips

✓ Treat ice-breaker questions seriously and practice your answers. They have more impact than many people realize.

✓ Pay attention to the style of the interviewer—if someone has a casual manner, your answers can be a bit more informal. But always remember that you're on the hot seat because you're the one being interviewed, so don't let your guard down.

✓ Make your answers long enough that the interviewer gets a sense of who you are. This impression is created by both what you say and how you say it.

✓ Don't get mad if you find yourself saying something that you think is "stupid." The point here is to engage in conversation, and it's unlikely that an interviewer will be bothered by a phrase that isn't as polished as you might have wished.

✓ Use your answers to this type of question to begin building your case: you are there to prove that you can do the job and do it well. Even talking about the weather or what school you went to allows you to get off to a good start. There are no innocent questions—and by that I mean the interviewer has an agenda and you will be evaluated by everything you say and do.

7

PRELIMINARY QUESTIONS

Now you're seated in the interviewer's office or a conference room and it's time for the interview to begin. As mentioned earlier, you can't be sure that your resume has been read or if the person interviewing you can answer detailed questions about the job. What you do know is that this is a high-stakes exchange and you want to impress this person that you're a good match.

You may have engaged in a little chitchat on the way to the office or conference room (see Chapter 6 on how to handle those "innocent" questions), but now you're in the warm-up pen and a curveball may be coming right at you. One of the most common preliminary interview questions is "Tell me about yourself." Here's a quick list of what not to include in your answer:

- ✓ Where you were born.
- ✓ A detailed career history.
- ✓ Why you're no longer with your past company.
- ✓ Personal information.

As we saw in Part I, your preparation is like a funnel or a road sign—it's telling you where to go with your answers. The first thought that should come into your head is something like, "What can I say about myself that proves I'm a good fit for this job?" Based on the job description and your research, you then start with what they're looking for:

- ✓ I'm an engineer with a broad background in manufacturing.
- ✓ I'm a biologist who has worked extensively in the lab focusing on....
- ✓ I'm an administrative assistant known for my ability to meet tight deadlines, and for my excellent attention to detail.

As you can see from these statements, they're mostly factual, but they may also begin the "sell" process. You have to decide, as part of your preparation, what is of most value to the interviewer(s). In the case of the engineer, it's breadth of background, and for the administrative assistant it's getting the work done. This is not an accident or you winging it—this initial statement is part of your plan. Now you've come to a fork in the road: ask a question (ZAP), or give an example. Let's look at a few questions first:

- ✓ Before I tell you more about my engineering background, would you mind explaining the major challenges you're having at your plant?
- ✓ I know this is a temporary position, but would I be supporting more than one manager?

Or, give an example of an accomplishment that hopefully hits the bull's-eye of their needs:

- ✓ My trademark as an engineer is cost-effective and creative solutions. When my most recent company couldn't figure out how to double production, they came to me and I figured out a three-part plan that met these aggressive goals.

✓ Many biologists at my level lose their bench skills, but as the team leader, I've always kept close to the research itself, which is what made me so successful.

✓ To reiterate: Say who you are (by function and level) that best matches what the company is looking for, and then either ask a question so that you know even more about what they want, or give an example that proves you're really good at your work. Let's look at some additional preliminary questions and how to answer them.

Why are you interested in this job?

+A. Your company is close to where I live and you have a good reputation. *Not a great answer, as where you live is not a selling point and "good reputation" is too general. It could apply to almost any company and tells the interviewer that you didn't bother to do your research.*

*A. I think it's a good fit. You're looking for an administrative assistant who can jump right in and help the office run more smoothly. That's what I'm good at. *A bit better, because here we have a few specifics, but watch the use of soft phrases like "I think." They often raise doubts in the interviewer's mind.*

!A. From what I know, your purchasing department is under tremendous pressure to keep up with the company's expansion. As an Administrative Assistant who recently helped XYZ go through a similar process, I'm confident I can make this easy for you as I'm organized and known for meeting tight deadlines. *This answer gives the interviewer solid evidence of the candidate's research, their past work experience, and their strengths, while also answering the question. In other words, this person is saying he or she would like to work here because the company has a challenge that they have met before and are confident they can meet again.*

What happened with your last company? Why aren't you still there?

+A. They acquired another company and my job was cut. *A bit too brief, this answer sticks to facts, which is good, but risks coming across as blunt.*

*A. It was a wonderful place to work and I enjoyed my 12 years there, but when the company decided to acquire its major competition, many jobs were cut including mine. *Better in tone, this answer gives a bit more detail and is upbeat.*

!A. As I'm sure you know, many IT jobs have been outsourced. I was lucky to remain with XYZ for 12 years, but when we lost a major contract, my position, along with many others, was eliminated. I'm excited to be looking for a new opportunity where I can use my project management skills to help run complex projects. *Giving the best explanation in a safe way—meaning in a way that has nothing to do with you or your performance—creates the strongest answer. And it's smart to end by linking job loss to your current search, along with a selling point.*

What do you think is the most important characteristic of an Underwriter?

+A. Well, you have to pay close attention to the details, evaluating the information provided in the application and following the corporate underwriting guidelines. I'm an attentive person who evaluates the data and follows the underwriting guidelines and that makes me a good Underwriter. *A somewhat vague answer, this doesn't do much to sell the candidate, even though the thoughts or concepts of the answer aren't bad.*

*A. An Underwriter must understand risk and the complexity of evaluating risk. For example, when I was starting out as an underwriter with The Hartford, my manager helped me see how critical it was to understand this fundamental part of the role. *This* *answer starts with a good, strong opening statement, but the example doesn't quite sell the concept as there are no specifics.*

!A. An Underwriter must understand risk and the complexity of evaluating risk. For example, while at The Hartford, I worked on a complicated marine account and I had to consider multiple issues to price the account, such as the replacement value of the yachts, the locations of the risk, the probability of hurricanes (the client was in Florida), and the use of the yachts. My first pricing estimate was flawed because I hadn't included an estimate for the wind exposure in Florida. By using some internally developed models for the pricing of the wind component, it helped me to understand the risk in a more robust way and led me to properly price the account, providing the insured with a policy that properly protected his assets. *Starting with the same opening phrase, this is the best answer, because the candidate explains step-by-step how he came to his conclusion. Remember: Facts or specifics are the most effective sales tools. If you don't have any work experience, then use what you've learned in school or from volunteering to give a similar answer.*

Through the Gauntlet

Gail was a graphic designer in the advertising business and was always well prepared. She had an interview scheduled with a local PR firm and was excited about it. She knew she would be meeting with the agency director, Rupert, but wasn't sure if anyone else would be involved. Here's how the interview started after a brief hello and being escorted into a conference room by the director who kept looking at his watch.

Rupert: Why do you want this job?

Gail: "I'm excited about your agency because you're a leader in pharmaceutical marketing. My whole career as a graphic designer has been in that segment and I know I could help you with innovative designs that meet your clients' needs."

Rupert: I don't have much time to talk with you. Are you better than the others I'm interviewing?

Gail: "That would be hard to say since I don't know who they are. Would you like to look at my portfolio? That will give you a better sense of what I can do for you."

Rupert: Okay.

Gail showed him several samples of her packaging designs and other work, giving a short explanation for each. She struggled not to feel insulted by his abrupt manner and fought her impulse to get up and leave the room. He sat in silence and didn't comment on her work.

Rupert: Can you stay late on a regular basis?

Gail: "What do you mean by late?"

Rupert: You know this industry; when we have a deadline, we can't go home. Several nights a week the team is here until 9 or 10 p.m. Is that a problem for you?

Gail was now tongue-tied. Not only was Rupert rude, but he was making demands that didn't fit with her other responsibilities. She gave it one last try.

Gail: "If you speak with my references, they'll tell you that I get the job done. I understand that the client comes first, but I'm not interested in a position where staying late is the norm. At my last firm, we discovered that if we gave our clients a realistic timeframe for their projects, we could avoid many of those stressful late-night sessions where few people are productive."

Rupert looked at his watch one more time, stood up, shook Gail's hand and left the room. The interview was over.

When Gail and I debriefed a few days later, she was laughing, and said to me, "How rude was that?" I agreed and told her that I thought she had done a wonderful job in a very tough situation. It was obvious that this particular agency was not dealing with their client demands in a way that would work for Gail. She recognized that it might work for others, but she knew herself well enough to see that this wasn't the job for her. In this case, the interview never made it past the preliminary questions.

Ditch It!

1. *Is this question related to the job?* This is a challenging question and is likely to make a bad situation worse. Even when asked an unreasonable or rude question, do your best to diffuse it. Remember: You might be able to use the rephrase technique from Chapter 4.

2. *I've never worked in this industry, so I can't answer that.* Try to avoid flat-out negative statements like this one. You can't lie, but see if there is something positive to say such as: "I'm excited about this industry because...." and fill in the blank. Your preparation will help you here.

3. *I've only worked for a small, family-run company, so I don't know how a large, international firm does business.* A critical part of your preparation is building a bridge from your current experience to what is needed for this particular job. Even if you haven't worked for a large firm, you probably have friends who do, or can find contacts on LinkedIn who can give you a quick tutorial that will help you answer this question more effectively.

Tips

- ✓ Take preliminary questions seriously. They form a crucial part of getting you to the next step, which is often the substance questions. Don't answer these questions as if they don't matter.
- ✓ Remember to ensure that your nonverbal language supports your answers. As discussed in Chapter 5, we believe what we see and hear, not words only. When under attack as Gail was, it's easy to slip into a defensive way of responding. Do your best to stay neutral and of course, you'll evaluate the interview after, and will decide that you don't want to work for someone who is rude, unless it was a test to see how you would react to stress.
- ✓ Practice giving examples when you speak to your friends and also use the ZAP technique or asking a question back in your everyday conversations. These two strategies will help you navigate through preliminary questions.
- ✓ Don't memorize your answers, but keep a running list of your best accomplishment stories. Many job seekers find it helps to categorize them so that if you've asked about how you resolved a conflict with your boss, you can pull this right off the list. You would also have some of these examples right on your interview MAP, too (Chapter 1).

8

SUBSTANCE QUESTIONS

You have finally arrived. After all your preparation and introductory questions, you're at the heart of the interview. What will happen? That's an impossible question to answer as there are too many variables. Some companies have a well-established process, while others let each hiring manager and HR staff create their own way to run interviews. But what I can say is that this is where the interviewer determines if you have the qualifications to do the job. And even if there are several more steps before you receive an offer, the substance part of interviews is make or break. This is when your task is quite simply to convince them that you can do the job and do it well.

In Part III where we look at types of interviews, you'll find many sample questions with "good, better, best" answers and a brief explanation (as you've seen in the past two chapters). Many of these questions fall into the substance category, but in this chapter we'll focus on:

✓ How to recognize substance questions.

✓ The best ways to answer them.

✓ What you can do if you're missing a key skill or qualification.

✓ How to make sure you've convinced the interviewer that you can do the job.

You recognize a substance question quite simply by its content. These questions are about the work you've done, the education and training you've received, or a qualification you have, boiling down to that essential: "Can you do this job?" Sometimes they're behavioral (Chapter 14) and other times they're open-ended and less structured.

The best way to answer any question is with specifics that follow a logical structure like PAR (problem, action, result). Adults like stories almost as much as children, as they pull us into someone else's world and allow us to see them in action. And the examples you give are carefully chosen to meet what the company or organization needs. So if you've got a great story about changing the way the billing was handled, but it's not relevant to the job you're interviewing for, then save it for another day, or see if you can use it for a question about creativity, problem-solving, and so on. And because interviewing is a conversation, you're going to ask for guidance along the way, including: asking questions, paying attention to the interviewer's body language, and using clarifying statements such as, "If I understand you correctly, you're changing the way your HR department is organized so that each area of the company will have its own representative. Is that right?"

When you're missing a key skill or qualification don't panic. You may be able to convince the interviewer that you are the right person for the job because you can learn quickly (and you offer evidence of this), and you're highly motivated and likable—communicated primarily through your body language, facial expression, and voice. Don't assume you know what the interviewer will decide. I had an interview years ago with the hiring manager of an outplacement firm after being downsized by the first outplacement firm I worked for. I was ushered into his office, he stood up and shook my hand, and pointed to the chair where I was to sit. He asked me a wide range of questions—almost all in the substance category—which I answered. But while this was going on a voice in my head kept repeating: "He hates me! I'll never get the job!" This was because he showed no emotion or reaction, no matter what I said. I subsequently nicknamed him *Stone Face*.

I couldn't shake the feeling that the interview was over, but did my best to remain upbeat and to answer his questions. At the end, with the same formality and lack of expression, he thanked me for coming in and I left. I was in a funk because I was sure I would never hear from this company again, but I sent my thank-you note anyway. Two days later my phone rang and it was the head of training for this company. She offered me the job and I burst out laughing. When she asked me why this was funny, I quickly explained that I hadn't received any sense from the interviewer (Stone Face) that he was interested in me as a candidate. The head of training then told me that he was so impressed with me that he had suggested they skip the second interview and bring me on board right away. I thanked her, set up a time to go over the details and negotiate, and got off the phone. Boy, was I wrong!

Before looking at sample substance questions and answers, how do you know if you've convinced the interviewer that you can do the job? Ask them and pay attention to their body language. Also, if you're asked if you're free to come in again to meet with the VP, then you have a clear sign that you're on the short list. What could I have asked Stone Face that might have kept me from thinking that all was lost? "Before I leave, could I ask you if you see me as a good fit for this position?" or "I'm very excited about joining your firm. Do you have any remaining questions about my ability to do this job and do it well?" These are typical wrap-up statements that we'll look at in Chapter 23.

Now let's look at substance questions and answers, remembering that these often come after the ice-breaker and preliminary ones.

Thanks, Al, for telling me about yourself. Why did you stay in pharmaceutical sales for so long when you also have an interest in marketing?

+A. I remained in sales to keep an accurate understanding of the customers I will eventually market products to. As I transition into marketing, I know that this "real world" view of how physicians respond to our products will ensure that my campaigns are effective. *Not a bad answer, this one makes it sound as if Al stayed in sales to get to know his customers, when in fact he may have stayed in sales because he was having a hard time making the transition to marketing. So while you build a bridge from where you've been to where you want to go, make sure your statements are accurate.*

*A. Even back in college I had an interest in marketing but was hired right after graduation by a leading pharmaceutical firm as part of their sales force. After several years and some very nice promotions, I invested in learning more about marketing because I wanted to do something new, and I thought that there would come a time when I no longer wanted to be a road warrior. Lastly, I don't see sales and marketing as two distinct functions as I believe they're closely related. What I bring to your company is both. *A bit better, this answer brings the two pieces together, but includes some risky information about getting tired of working in sales.*

!A. Did my career in sales keep me from working in marketing? (Note: This is a rephrase and Al is not expecting an answer from the interviewer.) Yes and no. I was fortunate to join XYZ right out of college as a sales rep, and throughout the next few years I managed major accounts. I think of this time as my basic training; I learned a great deal about cardiovascular drugs and how to interact effectively with physicians. One of my mentors, a boss, kept telling me that I would also be good in marketing, so I've taken several courses throughout the years and recently joined an international pharmaceutical marketing association. This is why I'm so excited about this position; it would allow me to use both my sales and marketing experience to help your company remain a leader in the field. *Using the powerful rephrase technique, Al sets up the question to his advantage and then answers it. His "yes and no" is interesting and he then explains what he means, ending with a strong sell to the interviewer.*

Can you give me an example of a risk you took at work and how things turned out? (This is a behavioral question. For more on this type of question, see Chapter 14.)

+A. Sure. My most recent boss thought we should use an outside vendor for our new training manual. Although I understood the cost savings, I was concerned about the quality and sent her a proposal that listed the pros and cons of using internal resources versus outside vendors. Although it didn't change her mind, I think she saw me as proactive and creative. *The specifics here are good, but the answer ends on a weak note with the "I think"; this would have been a stronger example if the boss had been persuaded to change her mind.*

*A. As director of marketing for a leading telecommunications firm, I was responsible for transforming the positioning of Global Services from traditional maintenance to a two-billion-dollar service business that enabled customers' migration to leading-edge technology. This was initially seen by management as too high a risk, but when I created a team of highly motivated individuals, recognized by customers, analysts, and channels for providing quality sales tools, virtual tours, ROI, and Business Impact Tools, they recognized that I was meeting our customers' business needs in a new and highly successful way. *Notice how this interviewee sets the stage—telling us where we are and then going into the details of the transformation. This is also a strong answer because it brings in outside opinions, offering proof from experts that this risk was worth taking.*

!A. Yes, I'd be glad to. Working in accounting, I'm trained to pay careful attention to the balance sheet, and several months ago I noticed some irregularities that I couldn't explain. I thought about it for a few days, did careful research, and then showed the problem to my boss. He said he'd take care of it, but a month later, the problem was unchanged. I emailed him, asking again for his help in resolving this, and I was once again told not to worry. I took a few more days to think about what I should do and finally made an appointment to meet with HR. I told them that I didn't know the cause of the problem and that this meeting had to be kept confidential, but that I didn't feel right ignoring the errors I was seeing. They went to the CFO and with her help were able to discover a glitch in our system. Getting this resolved not only corrected our books, but also kept us clean for any upcoming audits. *What do we learn about this candidate from this example? That he is highly accurate, ethical, and an excellent problem-solver. He also demonstrates courage, as he took a risk in going to HR. And he ends his story with excellent benefits to the company—a winning wrap-up.*

Why should we hire you as a teacher when you've spent your whole career working in financial services?

+A. Kids need to learn about the real world—not just book learning—and with my hands-on experience of how good mathematical skills can lead to high-paying jobs, I'm the right one to teach your advanced high school math classes. *This answer takes two big risks: using informal language like "kids" and making an assumption about what education should include. Although this may be true, if the candidate is being interviewed by a school superintendent, he or she may not be swayed by the lure of "high-paying jobs."*

*A. What I've learned over my extensive career in financial services will help me be a better math teacher. I know how to explain highly complicated processes to diverse audiences and can help students—both honors and the regular classes—get excited about it. Many students see math as abstract and divorced from day-to-day life, but I can bring what I've experienced in my corporate work to show them not only how useful it is, but also how math is a critical part of a good education. *A bit better, this answer starts to build the bridge from the candidate's past to the job at hand.*

!A. What value would my corporate background bring to the students I teach? (Here is a rephrase, used as the question is somewhat negative or challenging. Notice how the word *value* starts to do the work of the answer.) As I went through the certification process, I've had the chance to both observe several high school math teachers and ask their advice. Most of the ones I spoke with were excited about the ways I could use my background in the classroom. My strength as a teacher is the same as my credentials in financial services—I'm a good problem-solver and excel at creative solutions. I'm certain my students will benefit from this and I'm confident I could be a good addition to your teaching staff. *Using other experts' opinions is a smart part of this answer and the ending is very strong as it connects the candidate's past with the math teaching position and benefits to the students. Remember: It's all about them.*

Give me an example of an innovation you made and how it helped your company? (Again, a behavioral question designed to find out how creative you are.)

+A. In my role as a Database Architect, there wasn't much room for innovation. I did my job and did it well, but it was the VP's role to look at the big picture and suggest improvements. *A weak answer, always try for some example that matches the question, even if it's something small.*

*A. As VP Data Warehouse Manager, I managed a team of five or six technical individuals implementing Business Objects as BI Reporting and performed as a Functional Lead for Data Warehouse Development. I conducted interviews and JAD sessions for gathering business requirements and conducted system demos and presentations. And then I convinced management to implement the Data Warehouse using the Data Bus Architecture. This new approach provided a robust and scalable Data Warehouse to support

BI Reporting. *Notice how powerful this answer becomes by taking the interviewer step-by-step through the candidate's experience.*

!A. I'd be glad to. When I look back over my career, innovation is the one thing that really stands out. When I was hired by XYZ, I used my in-depth technical background to identify data sources for our data warehouse environment, and resolved data integration issues across applications and technical infrastructures. This saved us time and money and had other repercussions as well. My boss stated in a recent review that my ability to seek better ways to do things was my winning trademark. *The strongest answer, this one starts and ends with statements that articulate the candidate's competitive advantage. In highly technical areas such as this one, many job seekers feel uncomfortable making "selling" statements about themselves and prefer to stick to technical lingo. If this applies to you, see if you can find a middle ground.*

Winning the Contract

Heather had decided to set up her own business using her extensive background in medical writing and pharmacovigilance services. As we worked on her marketing and interview strategy, I learned that she had become a medical writer on her own. While working with her previous company, they had hired freelancers to do this work, and after a few years of editing the results, Heather realized she could do a better job than they did. She convinced her boss to let her try it and was a huge success. But as she anticipated going on interviews, she was worried that her credentials might not be enough to persuade a company to use her services.

As we worked on her competitive advantage as an entrepreneur, she realized that she had two major selling points: the breadth of her background and her ability to provide expert guidance and quality documents. She created a brochure to help sell her services and listed critical points such as her in-depth understanding of FDA and global safety regulations. But

she knew that the real "sell" would come from meeting with potential clients—really an interview that focused on substance.

I asked her to create a list of "nightmare questions"—ones
that she hoped she would never be asked—as well as more
routine ones that focused on what a biotech or pharmaceutical
company would need to know to hire her. We practiced these
questions and Heather used her "show and tell"—samples of
the documents that she had written at work (with proprietary
information deleted)— to make her pitch even more convincing.

Through a networking contact, she met with the senior
team at a mid-size pharmaceutical firm, and by sharing her passion for this work as well as proof of her abilities, they hired her
on a trial basis to work on a small project. Before long this ex-
panded into a much larger contract that is still ongoing. Heather found that her careful preparation for substance questions
and her brochure that listed her range of services did the job.
And it was interesting that no one ever asked her how she had
become a medical writer.

Ditch It

1. *Good question* or *That's a good question.* This statement
   creates a problem as most interviewers will recognize
   it as a stalling technique, and it can also make them
   wonder why you didn't say that their other questions
   were good, great, wonderful, terrific, and so on. If you
   need time to think, say so, but avoid this trap.

2. *I never did that before.* Of course you're going to be
   honest, but at the same time you've got to be smart.
   When asked about something you've never done, you
   might want to ZAP or ask a question back. You could
   say, "I'm not familiar with that. Could you tell me a
   bit more about it?" and hope that there is something

in the explanation that allows you to build a bridge between what you've done and what they want.

3. *I already told you that I know how to do that!* Getting annoyed is a quick way to end an interview. You will politely offer to explain your background as many times as necessary, but if you're confused by a question, you can ask: "I'm sorry, I'm not sure I understood that. Could you repeat it please?"

Tips

✓ Learn to recognize substance questions and provide the interviewer with details of your work. Give examples when you can that follow the PAR (problem, action, result) structure.

✓ Ask a question if you're not sure what the interviewer wants.

✓ Pay attention to your physical skills and watch the interviewer(s) carefully to make sure your answers are long enough to give them the information they need, but not so long as to be boring and to take away their control of the process.

✓ Even where you failed or the results weren't what you had hoped, demonstrate what you learned from the experience and stay upbeat.

✓ It's okay to tell an interviewer that you don't know the answer to a question, but try to add the steps you would take to get the answer.

✓ If your mind goes blank and you can't remember a date or fact or other piece of information, stay calm and glance down at your interview MAP. If it's not on your MAP, tell the interviewer that you can't recall that right now, but will of course remember it on the way home and will include it in your thank-you note. It's all right to be human. As I tell my clients, "You're not a walking encyclopedia."

9

FIT QUESTIONS

Here we are at the point in interviewing that is more magic than science. What is "fit"? I think of it as the moment when the interviewer thinks to him/herself—"She could work out. I like her," or "He's really motivated. He might fit in really well with our team." Your feelings count too, but because you're not the one making the hiring decision, we'll focus on how to help interviewers see you as a good fit.

Any question could end up being a "fit question" whether ice-breaker, preliminary, substance, behavioral, or combative. You might be asked about the latest book you've read, if you like to cook, where you volunteer, or whether you have a cat or a dog. Although you may be thinking to yourself, "What does this have to do with the job I'm interviewing for?" the interviewer is figuring out if you'll be easy to integrate into the company, department, team, or what you'll be like as an individual contributor. In Chapter 5 we looked carefully at how to make a good first impression, but with "fit" we have to go beyond that. Here are a few pointers to keep in mind:

- ✓ Learn to recognize fit questions and make sure you understand the core issue or what the interviewer is looking for before you answer.
- ✓ Ensure that your nonverbal communications (posture, gesture, eye contact, facial expression, and voice) support your positive message about yourself even when you're not sold on the job.
- ✓ Don't be thrown by what may feel like a detour or an irrelevant question. Have the attitude that if they asked it, you'll answer it, unless it's an illegal or insulting question.
- ✓ Keep your overall communications strategy in mind even while talking about your hobbies. I, for example, love to kayak. What does that tell an interviewer about me? That I'm adventurous, love being outside, and have a bit of physical stamina. So while kayaking isn't part of the job description, I may try to use it to "sell" these broader personal attributes related to my hobby (willing to try new things, not afraid of risk, young at heart).

Level of interest is related to fit and has two sides—their interest in you and yours in them. How can you judge their level of interest?

- ✓ Nonverbal signs, such as leaning forward, facial expressions, eye contact.
- ✓ The questions they ask—when the interviewer gets into more detail about the position.
- ✓ A change in schedule—you were going to meet only one person and now you'll meet three.
- ✓ A request for another meeting—or if the initial step is a phone interview, a request for a first meeting.
- ✓ A tour of the facility.
- ✓ Paperwork—you're asked to fill out an application or other forms such as the I-9.
- ✓ A request for your references.
- ✓ Questions about your availability.

And to turn it around, how do interviewers know your level of interest?

- ✓ Again, your nonverbal language.
- ✓ The quality of your answers.
- ✓ A willingness to clear your schedule.
- ✓ Positive comments about the company.
- ✓ Taking care of the paperwork promptly and accurately.
- ✓ Providing references.
- ✓ Giving the interviewers the impression that they are the most important thing in your life (okay, that's a bit dramatic, but telling them that they are your first choice).

Remember, we determine level of interest all the time when we bump into a neighbor or meet someone new or participate in a meeting at work. This is not like learning a foreign language—it's really just paying attention to the language you already know. Also, keep in mind that the company wants to hire someone to do this job and they'd be very glad if it's you as long as you have the skills and abilities they require. All you have to do is prove that you're a good fit, provide detailed answers with a selling point, and show interest in the job as well as in the people interviewing you.

Lastly, don't confuse the interviewer or interviewers with the job. Because we know first impressions can be inaccurate, do your best to stay neutral. Your job is to sell yourself, to prove you're a good match for what they need. That's it. Pay attention to what you learn in the process, but don't make a decision during the interview, and don't let someone's style or nervousness in conducting an interview deter you from finding out enough to make a good decision. This is a one-step-at-a-time process. It's not useful to jump to a conclusion when you're barely in the door. I can't tell you how many clients I've coached who had negative first impressions about a company and then ended up loving the job. Let's look at some fit questions and analyze the best ways to answer them.

What do you do, Ralph, to stay current in your field?

+A. Well, I read a lot and I'm active in a few LinkedIn groups for procurement professionals. *Ralph is not helping himself here with an answer that is too casual and too short. And while this question has a substance component, it is more likely a question about motivation. In other words, does Ralph just do the minimum to get by, or is he someone who does more than what is required?*

*A. To stay current, I go beyond the 20 hours of yearly mandatory training and have enrolled in several online courses that I complete after work. The value of this is that I'm connected to procurement professionals outside of my company. This helps me do a better job. *Here, Ralph gives a concrete example of what he does and its value, as he addresses the key issue of motivation.*

!A. Just recently I organized a conference at work, bringing in outside procurement professionals, so that we could review our best practices and make sure our company policies keep us in the forefront. At first my boss thought this wouldn't be productive, but I was able to give him specific evidence of the ways we could use this information to keep our costs down. This was so successful that he asked me to help other regions follow our example. I also read widely in industry journals and am active in my professional association. I know that what I invest in myself has direct benefits for the company I work for. *Here, Ralph does a better sales job of showing how he overcame resistance, including results, and used a great tie-back to remind the interviewer what he or she will gain from this highly motivated candidate.*

Can you describe a really difficult decision you had to make and how you handled it? (A classical behavioral question that can be used to determine fit.)

+A. The most difficult decision I had to make was whether or not to stay with XYZ when I had an offer from another company.

The boss I had reported to for five years joined a new company, and after a few months he recruited me to join him. I was really torn because I was responsible for a team and didn't feel I should leave them. I stayed, but then six months later lost my job. *While this answers tells a story, it doesn't reveal enough about the decision-making process to provide the interviewer with a good sense of what makes him or her tick, and it ends on a down note leading the interviewer to the conclusion that this person made a mistake.*

*A. The most difficult decision I had to make was whether or not to stay with XYZ when I had an offer from another company. I hadn't been looking to leave, but my boss of five years asked me to join him at the new company where he was working. I made up a pros and cons list, sought advice from a few trusted advisors, and came to the conclusion that, although the new opportunity had some clear benefits, I wasn't ready to leave my current situation. *A stronger answer, this one shows how the job candidate made the decision and makes him sound both loyal and smart.*

!A. I've made many difficult decisions throughout the course of my career, but one I struggled with was whether or not to leave my company when my former boss recruited me. She and I had a wonderful relationship and under her guidance I had tripled our sales in the Northeast. But when I thought about it carefully and looked at the new sales initiatives I had just launched with XYZ, I decided to stay. Because I shared with her how hard it was to say no, and by telling her that I would be thrilled to work with her again, I didn't burn any bridges and she has remained a close advisor. Just two months after I made this decision, I was promoted to VP—a very nice confirmation of the value I bring to XYZ. *This answer addresses the core issue of how this candidate made a tough decision, and in the process proves the value he brought to his company. He also describes how effectively he maintains important relationships. Adding the promotion at the end puts the icing on the cake—this is validation that he made a good choice.*

Can you tell me, Cynthia, what your coworkers would say about your ability to be an effective team member?

+A. Sure. Be glad to. In my last two positions at leading beverage firms, I led several teams and served on others. My coworkers would say I'm dependable. If I say I'm going to do something, I do it. And I park my ego at the door. *Although it gives an example, this answer is too general and Cynthia leaves out the tie-back, which would make it more convincing.*

*A. In my most recent review, one of the things my manager commented on was my outstanding teamwork. She was told by my coworkers, "Cynthia is the kind of person you can really depend on." I enjoy teamwork, as I've seen over and over again how a good idea can evolve into a great one with the input of different perspectives. My coworkers would also say I'm fair and a good listener. These are qualities I'm excited to bring to my next position. *Using her review and what her coworkers would say about her, Cynthia builds a more convincing case with this answer and strong tie back.*

!A. When I look back over my career, I realize I've changed as a team member—more specifically in what I think makes an effective one. When I started out in the beverage industry, we had weekly staff meetings as well as meetings for various subgroups. And it was hard to see the value of these meetings, because often not much was accomplished. But as I was promoted and started leading meetings myself, I came to see how important it was to gather diverse opinions before creating a plan. It was this input from all perspectives that often made an idea turn into a winning strategy for the company. So my coworkers would say I'm committed to our teams, I'm a careful listener, and I make a point to draw out everyone's opinion so that quiet team members also get a chance to speak. Given the awards that I've received for my initiatives, I'm confident that I owe much of that to the teams I've led. *In this excellent answer we get a story: how Cynthia disliked teams and how she grew into an important role as team leader. Keeping the essence of this fit question in mind, Cynthia ends by giving credit to her teams for the awards she has won. That's a "Wow!"*

Misfit

Sometimes, despite your best efforts, you will find yourself in a situation where the company's needs overshadow your career goals. In other words, they see you as a perfect fit and are ready to hire you on the spot, although you have many questions and feel as if you may be going down the wrong road.

Greg was in HR and had a broad background as a generalist. He had worked for several different industries, most recently in cosmetics. He was what I like to call a "mature" worker, meaning that he had worked for a long time and was fortunately not under financial pressure. During our meetings he made it clear that although he wasn't ready to retire, he wanted to work in ways that would allow him more free time and flexibility. He was particularly excited about his garden in New Jersey and both he and I had to be careful not to spend our entire sessions talking about compost and heirloom tomatoes.

Through a networking contact Greg was introduced to the HR Director at a leading cosmetics firm in New York. What surprised both of us was how quickly things escalated from introduction to interview. He had emailed the head of HR on a Monday, was called that day about meeting with her and one other senior person on Thursday. As we prepared for the meeting/interview, I asked Greg what he wanted. At first he laughed and said, "Not a job in New York! There goes my garden." Then as we talked about it, he realized that there were several advantages to this meeting: understanding the HR issues of another company, exploring contract or part-time work, getting referrals to other HR people to talk with, and interview practice. As an experienced HR generalist, Greg knew that it was impossible to predict what might happen, but he felt confident, because he had a plan. (Note: Greg couldn't create an interview MAP as there was no job description, but he did careful research on both the company and the two people he would be meeting with and brought in a list of questions.)

What happened surprised both of us. The HR Director seemed rushed and distracted. After thanking Greg for coming in she asked him if he was ready to fill out the paperwork that this company's parent company required. He politely asked if this could wait until they had a chance to understand each other's needs better, but the HR Director replied that they had a huge new contract that was going to require bringing in many new hires in the region and that she didn't have more than a few minutes to spend with him. She then delegated the rest of the meeting to the senior HR manager and walked out.

Greg did his best to compose himself and asked the HR Manager if he could please clarify what they were looking for. It turned out to be contract work that would start immediately, and the compensation, which was a required field on the form, was about one third of what he had been earning. The job also involved extensive travel. Realizing that this wasn't going to work for him, Greg asked if he could help them in a more strategic role that would use his extensive experience and give him the flexibility he wanted. The HR Manager told Greg that he wasn't the one who could make that decision. They shook hands, Greg got his card and the HR Director's, and left the building. He felt as if he'd been hit by a tornado. When we debriefed a few days later, Greg told me that he felt guilty for not being excited by this opportunity.

"But it isn't what you told me you wanted. Correct?" I had asked.

"I know, but it's a job, and although the pay is terrible and it would mean working 10 to 12 hour days, I wonder if something is wrong with me."

As we talked through this, Greg saw how important it was that he had a clear, written goal for his job search, and in this instance, his agenda had been overshadowed by the company's needs. In the end, rather than feeling guilty about it, he told me that he felt good that he had not caved—that he had stood up for what he wanted at this special time in his life. I shared with him something I learned from a friend of mine who has worked on a freelance basis most of her career, and that is if you accept a job like the one Greg walked away from, it can undermine your self-esteem and make it harder to get to the work you want.

Ditch It

1. *Since there isn't any written job description, how can I know what you want?* This isn't a smart question, because it's your job to figure out what they want. Some of this you can do before the interview through your research. But much of it will happen in the interview itself. Listen carefully, ask good, probing questions and be prepared for surprises. You'll find out what they want.

2. *I really don't know what my boss would say about my teamwork. She was never in the office.* Bells should be going off in your head when you hear an answer like this one. Although this may be true, it sure isn't helping you "sell" yourself. Your job is to come up with a positive statement that is accurate. But let's say you don't want to use your most recent boss because you didn't get along. Then you could say "I've chosen someone else to talk about my teamwork because they had the day-to-day exposure to my work and can give you more details."

3. *I can fit in anywhere!* Although this may be almost true, I don't think it would convince most people. You

aren't suited for every job out there and neither am I. The sidebar gives a good example of how important it is to know what you want and the environments that are going to create that all important win-win: you're happy and the company gets what they need.

Tips

✓ Pay attention to the essence of fit: Are you going to integrate well into the company? Do you bring in a much-needed skill? What are you going to be like to work with?

✓ As with other answers, follow a logical structure and provide specifics.

✓ Remember that your body language holds a majority vote: the way you look and how you sound are more convincing than the actual words you use.

✓ Approach interviews with an open mind. In your research you may have uncovered some problems or issues that make you wonder if this is a good place to work. Ask probing questions, listen carefully, pay attention to the interviewers' nonverbal signals, and don't make a hasty decision. A place that a friend of yours hates may be just perfect for you.

✓ Here is the essence of fit in list form: show the company you can do the job, will do the job, will fit into the organization, and highlight likability—you are one of "us."

✓ Stick to your plan but be flexible as long as you stay true to the basics of your objective. It's okay to walk away from something that's not the right fit—as long as your finances allow it. And because it can take time to get an offer that meets your goals, keep your pipeline full—you can't count on opportunities until you have a solid offer.

10

OTHER QUESTIONS

When I was in college, many of my friends were addicted to the TV series *The Twilight Zone*. It was a wonderful mixture of fantasy, science fiction, and horror based on deep psychological issues. As we wrap up looking at the types of questions, prepare to enter *The Twilight Zone*, as strange things can happen. I worked with a client several years ago whose interview didn't just include personal questions, it had nothing but this type of question for the entire interview. He was asked about what book he was reading, what he did for fun, how he resolved personal conflict, what he did to "restore" himself, how he spent his vacations, if he volunteered, whether or not he liked to cook, and if he'd agree to go on a rock climbing expedition.

Why did the interviewer do this? My educated guess is that this hiring manager placed a very high importance on who the candidate was (he was more interested in his personality than his accomplishments) and that possibly he'd been burned in the past by hiring someone who looked really good (strong resume, great accomplishment examples), but who turned out to be the wrong person for the job. Interviewers bring their hiring experience to the table and this may influence what happens in the interview. Also, remember that hiring the wrong person is a costly mistake: it takes months to fix and can have many negative repercussions.

It's flattering to have an interviewer interested in who we are, how we think, and what makes us tick, but when that crosses the line, it's time to end the interview. Let's set a few guidelines before we look at how to answer these rare questions from *The Twilight Zone*. Interviewers shouldn't:

- ✓ make personal comments that are flirtatious or sexual.
- ✓ touch you inappropriately (a handshake is fine, but anything else is unacceptable).
- ✓ ask about your marital status and if you have children (these are illegal).
- ✓ discriminate based on your race, religion, heritage, or sexual preferences (also illegal).
- ✓ drop the "f" bomb (take a look at the sidebar for a funny story about that one).
- ✓ insult you (but the combative style comes very close).
- ✓ throw your resume on the floor (this happened to me years ago).
- ✓ attack your credentials (basically calling you a liar).
- ✓ embarrass you in front of a group (often part of an intimidation technique, sometimes used to see how you respond to stress).

There may be other things to add to this list, but this will at least give you a start. What steps can you take when addressing these questions?

- ✓ Look for any links to substance—if you're asked about a book you've read, can you tie that to anything in the job description or your credentials?
- ✓ Use the rephrase technique (Chapter 4) to neutralize negative questions.

✓ Ask the interviewer why he or she asked you that (but be careful that your body language is open and non-combative).

✓ Protect yourself—if an interviewer's behavior is crossing the line, tell him or her that this is making you uncomfortable.

✓ Demonstrate your flexibility by answering questions that may be a bit out there, but don't feel compelled to answer illegal questions.

✓ Show you can talk about personal issues such as volunteer work or sports and use these to "sell" your strong personal attributes such as curiosity, generosity, honesty, and so on.

✓ Watch your initial reactions—if an interviewer is testing you by asking one of these "other" questions, you don't want to hastily decide that this is a horrible place to work. Pay attention, don't let anyone abuse you, and do your best to stay calm and professional. To use a great phrase from *The Dog Whisperer*: try to be "calm assertive."

Let's look at how to answer some of these far out questions.

Thanks for coming in today, Bruce. Can you give me four reasons why I shouldn't hire you?

+A. No, I really can't. I see my background as a great fit. *Although honest, this isn't a strategic or well-thought-out answer.*

*A. Sounds as if you're handing me a loaded gun and asking me to shoot myself in the foot! Why would I do that? *Way too combative, Bruce is most likely making the interviewer quite uncomfortable. And using guns as an analogy is not a good idea unless you're trying to work for the NRA.*

!A. Well, that's an unusual question! I'm sure I'm going to fail at this, but let me give you a list of a few things you might have questions about and then I'm going to tell you why you should hire me anyway. I've worked for only one company my entire career. You might think this limits me, but from my perspective, it shows that I was able to grow in a number of ways. I'm proud to say that I took on any challenges given to me and made a difference and can do the same for your company. I came into this industry in an unusual way. I majored in chemistry in college and never dreamed I'd end up in the food industry. But of course, having a chemistry background has given me a good foundation. *To keep this answer short, I'm not going to go through the other two items on Bruce's list, but you get the idea. By telling the interviewer that the question is an unusual one, Bruce is setting it aside and putting it in a category of its own. He then admits up front that he is going to "fail," because he can't come up with four reasons they shouldn't hire him. But to show he's a good sport, he gives examples and plays along.*

You've got lovely eyes, Laura. I'm going to move so that I can sit closer to you. (Yes, this really happened to a client of mine about a year ago. The interviewer, we'll call him Mark, moves to the chair right next to Laura and leans his shoulder on hers.)

+A. What on earth are you doing? *While understandable, Laura has escalated the situation and is basically counterattacking.*

*A. I don't think that's such a good idea. *A weak response, someone like Mark will probably ignore her.*

!A. Mark, this is a bit too close and you're making me uncomfortable. Would you mind sitting across the table from me? *Assertive yet calm, this response should get Mark to stay on his side of the table. If it doesn't, it's time for Laura to politely thank him for his time and leave.*

It's been great talking with you, Beth. Before we get to the last details, can you tell me if you have children?

+A. I've enjoyed our talk, too. What do children have to do with this job? *Blunt and to the point, this answer risks alienating the interviewer.*

*A. I'm really impressed by what you've shared with me today and I'm excited to join the company. Can we move ahead into the details? *Here Beth tries ignoring the illegal question to see if she can get the interviewer to move on without her answer. In some instances this could work.*

!A. Thanks, George. I'm so impressed by the high standards you and your company adhere to and I'd be very excited to be part of your team. If you talk with my references or coworkers you'll find out that I'm an open book—I don't have secrets. But I'm not sure how the question you've asked me relates to the job. Could you help me understand that? *Beth is using a ZAP or question back at the end to get out of a tight spot. She doesn't tell George that his question is illegal, but rather asks him a question—a soft way to challenge why he has asked it. And by telling him that she is an open book, she is really saying that once you get to know her, she can talk about more personal issues.*

Why would I hire someone like you who obviously can't stay with a company more than a year? (When you hear a negative question like this one I hope you're remembering Chapter 4 and the rephrase technique.)

+A. It wasn't my fault that I was let go several times. It happens to almost everyone. *This poor answers draws on pity—never a good idea.*

*A. I know my track record may give you concern, but what I'd like you to focus on is what I've learned from my experience and how I can help your company. *Not a bad way to start the answer, this example doesn't provide any proof that might turn the interviewer around.*

!A. What is it about the diversity of my experience that could be an advantage for your company? (This is a rephrase so the job candidate is not expecting an answer from the interviewer.) When I started out in a junior sales role at X, I had a wonderful mentor who taught me how critically important it is to listen to customers. When he moved on to Y, he recruited me and I followed him, moving up into a more senior role. Unfortunately, that company was bought out and both of our positions were eliminated. I then went on to Z and would still be there, but when they acquired their top competitor, many positions were cut, including mine. This somewhat rocky road has exposed me to the different ways companies do business and it's taught me ways to solve difficult problems and save money. So although working for different companies isn't what I would have chosen, I'm confident that my experience will help the next organization I work for. *Here is the power of the rephrase, because it turns a negative question into an opportunity to demonstrate competitive advantage. It's magical the way these rhetorical questions work—setting the stage for a strong answer with a selling point. Notice how the tie-back at the end strengthens the answer.*

You say you're PMP certified, but from what you've told me so far, I'm not sure you could manage a project out of a paper bag!

A+. If you look closely at my resume, you'll see that I've been instrumental in several large projects. *I know by now you don't need me to add anything here, but for the record I'll say don't refer to your resume and make sure to provide proof or examples. Otherwise your answers are weak.*

*A. At my last company, I received three awards for projects I managed. One was for completing a complicated project ahead of time, a second was for significant cost savings, and the third was for leading a large, international team. *Much better, this answer needs a tie-back to really address this attack.*

!A. How good are my project management skills? That's my favorite topic and let me tell you why. Five years ago I earned my PMP certification—an arduous process as you know. But the real benefit came as I applied what I had learned and was recognized with three awards for projects I managed. One was for completing a complicated project ahead of time, a second was for significant cost savings, and the third was for leading a large, international team. This was great affirmation of my project management skills—skills that I believe can help your company. Is there anything more specific that I can tell you that will put your mind at ease? *Here we have a rephrase and a ZAP—the answer starting and ending with a question. Remember: Questions are one of your most powerful interview tools—use them wisely and you can deal with almost any situation.*

The "F" Bomb

Henry was a senior manager with a strong background in logistics. He had started his career with an electronics company and was recruited many years later by a telecommunications firm. When sales hit a low point, he was let go and started his program with me. What I noticed about Henry, right from the start, was that he had a sparkle in his eye and seemed to enjoy life, no matter what happened. He wasn't happy about his job loss, but as a big, former defensive football player, it took a lot to shake him.

After about a month, Henry went on one interview, and after weeks of waiting for feedback, he learned that the company had selected an internal candidate. A few weeks later, he had several, high-level networking meetings that picked up his spirits—he was confident something would come from them. As we talked about the different ways to look for work, he decided to target a small firm that made products for the hospitality industry. He researched them carefully and crafted a strong target email to the CEO. Two days later he received a phone call from the CEO's administrative assistant saying he had an interview the following week.

The CEO was built like Henry and had a wild sense of humor. The first thing he told Henry was that he was amazed at how he had been able to make it to the CEO level "as a fat guy." He then smiled at Henry and said, 'You're f...ing big too!"

Henry laughed and said he had to be careful not to sit on small chairs. He was surprised by this executive's language, but liked his warm, no-nonsense style. As the interview continued, however, the CEO used the "f" bomb in almost every sentence and Henry felt a bit uncomfortable. He was careful to keep his answers free of swear words, but wondered if the CEO thought he was a prude.

At the end of the interview, the CEO gave him a huge bear hug and told him that he was "F...ing amazing."

Henry shook his hand, thanked him, got into his car, and burst out laughing. How crazy was that? When he and I debriefed, we had a good laugh as we realized this was a perfect example of how unpredictable interviews can be. Henry wrote a polite and detailed thank-you note to the CEO and kept his search going.

Before he heard back from the company, his first employer, the electronics firm, decided to hire him back. Henry and I reviewed the issues he wanted to negotiate and discussed whether or not he wanted to go back to the CEO of the small firm before accepting. With a twinkle in his eye he said to me, "No f...ing way!"

After a few months back with the electronics firm, Henry emailed me to say that things were going really well. The company had bridged his former service and valued the experience he had gained in the interim. Although glad that his search was over, Henry realized that he had benefited from the process by redefining his goals and by learning what other companies wanted. He also knew how to run a good search and had a stronger network in place to support himself for the rest of his career. As we wrapped up, he and I agreed he would probably never have an interview like this one again!

Ditch It!

1. *You can't ask me that! It's illegal.* Although you are correct, this isn't the smartest way to handle an illegal question. Think of using a question such as: "I'm not sure I see how this issue relates to the job. Could you help me understand that?"

2. *I'm protected by the Americans With Disabilities Act and you have to provide a reasonable accommodation.* Hostile again, this isn't a good way to go. But knowing your rights and which questions are illegal is very smart—just use that information in a more collaborative way.

3. *How did you become a senior manager with such a gutter mouth?* As we saw in the sidebar, you may run into an interviewer who uses colorful language. Be very careful not to slip into using it yourself, and if it bothers you, take time after the interview to figure out if this is a person you could work with.

Tips

✓ Know your rights: Title VII of the Civil Rights Act prohibits discrimination on the basis of gender, race, religion, or national origin. The more recent Americans

With Disabilities Act requires employers to provide equal opportunity for disabled workers and to provide reasonable accommodations.

✓   Use the rephrase technique to turn a strange or unusual question to your advantage.

✓   Prepare for the unexpected. The main reason I keep stressing strategy is that there is no way to anticipate what will happen in interviews. There are too many variables. But if you have skills or techniques that support effective strategies, you'll be prepared for anything.

✓   Remember to use your judgment, because you may decide it's just fine to tell an interviewer how old you are or what country your parents came from. Some interviewers know these questions are illegal and ask them anyway, and others aren't up on the laws and don't know they shouldn't ask them. The determining factors for you should be: Do you want this job and is the question being used as a way to eliminate you from the running? If it's not and you're comfortable answering the question, go ahead.

✓   In some instances you can use humor to deflect strange or illegal questions with a phrase like, "Oh, that's a surprise! I didn't think you could ask me that. Can you help me understand what you need?" And make sure that your body language, especially your facial expression, is open and friendly.

PART III

TYPES OF INTERVIEWS

11

PHONE SCREENINGS: YOU ARE WHAT THEY HEAR

Before we get into the phone interview, I'd like to share a few important bits of related advice. Let's say you're at the grocery store picking up a few items before the kids get home from school. Your cell phone rings and it's a number that you don't recognize. Should you answer the phone? Probably not, because if it's a recruiter, agency, or someone from HR calling to set up a phone screening, you don't want to sound rushed, distracted, and possibly unprofessional. Let the call go to voice mail and deal with it once the groceries are put away, the kids are quiet, and you can focus on the call.

The funniest example of when not to take a call came from a client of mine who was anxiously waiting for a recruiter to call him back. They'd had an initial conversation a few days earlier and the job was a perfect fit. He was in the shower when the phone rang, and without thinking, he turned off the water, jumped out dripping wet, and ran to the phone in his bedroom. He hadn't even taken the time to grab a towel. It was the recruiter and he ended up having a 15-minute conversation while he shivered and got the rug all wet. And while he felt he did all right, he was distracted and not at his best. So don't let your anxiety about getting the job make you answer your phone without thinking. And if this makes you feel better, you can tell potential interviewers to "Please leave a message on my cell phone and I'll call them back promptly."

What should your voice mail say? "This is Jean Baur at 555-555-5555. Please leave me a message and I'll get back to you as soon as I can. Thank you." And that is it. No music, no children's voices, no gimmicks. It's safer to stay away from religious messages, too. I have a few clients who add to their message things like: "Have a blessed day" or "God bless you." The intent is good, but it's risky during a job search. I suggest you go with the vanilla greeting and then, once you're hired, you can do anything you want on your voice mail.

You also need to plan where you'll be during a phone screening interview. It must be a quiet place where you have room to spread out your paperwork, which includes your resume, the job description, research on the company, your MAP (Chapter 1) and your prepared questions for them (included at the bottom of the MAP). And if you've written out your accomplishment statements or top achievements, you might want them handy too. Think about possible distractions and do your best to minimize them.

If you have a headset (and that's a good investment because it leaves your hands free and you won't get a headache from pressing the phone to your ear), put it on, plug it into your phone, don't use a cell phone unless you have no alternative, and be ready for the call. Look over your notes while you wait and make sure you also have a glass of water in case your allergies kick in or you start to cough. Have a pen, too, because you're going to take notes—first on your MAP, and if you need more space, on a pad of paper. If you need more guidance, read *The Essential Phone Interview Handbook* by Paul J. Bailo. It will help you make the best possible impression and get to the next step. Let's look at some typical phone screening questions and ways to answer them.

Are you still with XYZ?

+A. No. I was let go a year ago. *Way too blunt, this answer gets the phone screening off to a bad start. Never volunteer how long you've been in transition.*

*A. No, I'm not. I had a great 10 years there, but due to a downturn in sales, many positions were eliminated, including mine. *A bit better, here we at least have a positive message.*

!A. Why did XYZ have to cut its sales force by 60 percent? As you may know, they lost a huge contract and had to trim the sales force. I was one of the ones impacted, but I'm excited to be looking for a new position where my strong sales background will help a company grow. *Using the rephrase technique, this answer is the best, because it's upbeat and quickly gets off the issue of no longer being with the former employer. Notice that while it does this, it also answers the question.*

What are the three kinds of resumes? (I was asked this just a few months ago in a phone screening interview.)

+A. Well, there are many ways to tailor resumes, but the two basic types are reverse chronological, functional, and academic CV. *Phone screeners often have a list of factual questions designed to test your subject matter expertise. This answer is okay, but a bit rambling.*

*A. The three major types of resumes are reverse chronological, functional, and there is also the academic CV. Would you like me to elaborate? *Using the ZAP technique at the end, this is a clear and concise answer.*

!A. The three kinds of resumes most often used are the reverse chronological, functional, and CV. The reverse chronological is the one used most, except in academia, where you see the CV. And functional resumes are helpful for career changers. There are other variations, too, where a job seeker adapts or tailors his or her resume to the job requirements. *This answer gives more detail and lets the interviewer see how knowledgeable this person is. In phone interviews pay close attention to what the interviewer wants. If it's rapid fire, the second answer would be better.*

Could you relocate for this position?

+A. I don't know. The ad didn't say anything about relocation. *Although honest, this answer isn't inspiring and could cause the interviewer to thank you and say goodbye.*

*A. What particular locations did you have in mind? *Not a bad idea to use a ZAP, but this is a hot potato answer because it's too short.*

!A. Relocation? I hadn't thought about that, but I'm open to what works for the company. Did you have any specific places in mind? *Using both a rephrase and a ZAP, this is the best answer because it keeps the door open without the candidate making any commitment.*

Why did you apply for this position?

+A. It looked like a good fit and I'm interested in your company. *This is too vague to be convincing.*

*A. I applied for the Financial Analyst position at your company because I have the skills and experience to do the job well. If you look at my resume, I've done everything you're asking for. *With a strong beginning, this answer relies on the information in the resume—rarely a good idea.*

!A. I applied for the Financial Analyst position at your company because you're one of the leaders in the field and I have the skills and experience to do the job well. From what I understand, you need an analyst with a broad and diverse background. This is exactly what I have. Are there any specific areas of my background that you're concerned about? *This is a home run, because the candidate ties his knowledge of the company to the critical "fit" issue and then ends with a ZAP to see if there is something in particular he needs to address.*

Shall We Dance?

"Hello? This is Jean Baur."

"Good morning, Jean. This is Beverly Smith from Excellent Recruiting."

"Thank you very much for calling me."

(Note: I've now done two things: set the tone for the call by thanking her, and stopped talking so that she is clearly in charge of the process. Don't let being uncomfortable with silence make you talk when it's not your turn.)

"Your background seems a very good fit for the training position. Could you tell me how you got into training?"

"Sure, I'd be happy to. Early in my career I taught writing at NYU and also designed writing workshops for diverse groups. These experiences helped me realize that I liked training. After careful research, I identified a number of training firms in New York City, where I was living at the time, and was most impressed by Communispond—a firm specializing in presentation skills and business writing as well as some other management courses. Because of my work as a writer and my teaching credentials, they saw me as a good fit for their needs. After only one year with the firm, I was asked to help revise the writing program, bringing it up to date, turning it from a two-day course to one day, and increasing sales by 45 percent in the first quarter."

"That's a good story. What makes you interested in our position?"

This is where all I have to do is look at my MAP and create an answer that shows I've done careful research on the company and can illustrate that magical thing we call "fit." In other words, I must prove that I have what they're looking for. But as we discussed earlier, I can't assume that the job description is either complete or accurate, so I might start my answer like this:

"If I understand your needs correctly, you want someone who can deliver existing programs to your clients while being aware of additional areas for development. (I have a choice here—I can ZAP and say something like, "Is that correct?" or, if I'm fairly certain that I am correct, I can then go into an accomplishment story or example that shows how I did this in the past.)

I then could add something specific about the company such as: "I'd really like to work with you because XYZ is a leader in the field. Your classes are relevant, practical, and up-to-date. And I'm particularly impressed by the choice of training options you offer including in-house classes, webinars, podcasts, and E-learning. This is a smart way to make your materials appropriate for different types of adult learners."

(What I've done here is show that I've done my homework. But I'm not mentioning these facts in a vacuum, I'm using them to carefully answer a specific question. Let's jump ahead now to how the call might end.)

"Thanks, Jean, for telling me about your background."

"You are welcome, Beverly. I'm very interested in this position and was wondering if you can tell me what the next steps might be?" (Note: By using "might," I'm avoiding presuming that I'm their candidate of choice.)

"We have a number of other candidates to screen and then we'll be inviting a few people in for the face-to-face interviews."

"Would it be all right if I follow up with you in about two weeks?"

"We'll be calling the people we want to move forward."

(I've now met resistance. Beverly obviously doesn't want me to call her, so if I insist on it, I'm probably doing myself more harm than good.)

"I understand. Thank you very much for speaking with me and I hope to hear from you. I'm excited about this position and know I could be a good addition as a trainer." (This is my wrap-up statement. See Chapter 23.)

"I've enjoyed speaking to you as well. Goodbye, Jean."

"Goodbye."

As you look at this sample of a phone screening, you should be able to see how all the preparation covered in Part I has paid off. I've done careful research on the company. I've studied the job description. I've made a MAP and have prepared questions to ask them. And I've practiced out loud so that this isn't the first time I've heard my own voice giving these answers. This doesn't mean, however, that there won't be surprises. In this example, the interviewer didn't want me to follow up. Rather than letting that throw me, I moved on and eventually wrote a polite email to Beverly that day reminding her of the main reasons why I'm the right candidate for the job and thanking her for her time. If I didn't hear back from her in 10 days to 2 weeks, I would email her again, figuring at this point that I have nothing to lose. (More on this in Chapter 25.)

Ditch It

1. *Well, um, I have, um, worked um in manufacturing, ah, well I guess, for like most, um, of, you know, my career.* Non-words, the "ums," "ahs," "likes," and "you knows" make us sound weak and uncertain. If you use them in your everyday speech, go on a non-word diet and enlist the help of friends, asking them to raise their hand every time you use one. Keep good eye contact

and don't be afraid of short pauses and you'll reduce your non-words.

2. *Yup.* A one-word answer is not helpful in any kind of interview. If they've asked you if you have a background in the food industry, in addition to yes, you need to provide details that could include how many years you've been in the industry as well as the companies you've worked for. Think of interview questions like a hot potato—the interviewer will not like you if you throw it back to them too soon, because they need time to listen to your answer and plan their next question.

3. *What? I can't hear you! What did you say?* If there is a poor connection or if the interviewer is difficult to understand, make sure you ask for help in a polite way. It would be much better to say, "I'm sorry. I didn't understand your question. Could you repeat it please?" But if after you've tried that a number of times and you still can't understand the interviewer, then it might be smart to suggest an alternative, such as calling on a land line, using Skype, or if practical, meeting in person.

Tips

- ✓ Prepare carefully for phone screening interviews. Never assume you can simply wing it.
- ✓ Make sure that you're in a quiet place with no distractions during phone interviews. Use a good quality phone, a head set, and turn off call-waiting or anything else that could break your concentration.
- ✓ Dress in something that's comfortable but not sloppy. PJ's or sweatpants don't make you feel as

professional as a nice pair of pants and a dress shirt.
Business casual works well for most people.

✓ Sit up straight, smile when appropriate, talk in a
normal volume, and if there are any reasons why you
might be difficult to understand (you have a bad cold
or English is not your first language) then make sure
to make it easy for the interviewer to ask for clarification.

✓ Ask at the start of the interview how much time
is allotted so that you're not surprised when the
interview is over. This allows you to include your top
accomplishment examples and give your wrap-up
statement.

✓ Train everyone in your household how to answer
the phone and take messages. Don't let your spouse
or children scream your name if they're the ones
answering the phone, because it creates a really bad
impression. Better yet, use your cell phone as your
job search number and your home phone for interviews.

✓ As my wonderful colleague Frank Harvey says, remember the purpose of the phone screen is to screen
you out. Make sure you convince the screener that
you belong on the "yes" list.

12

HR SCREENING: ARE YOU A MATCH?

My clients often ask me why they have to go through an HR screening, often conducted by phone, but sometimes in person. The easy answer is that HR serves as a gatekeeper and is helping busy hiring managers with a preliminary but critical part of the hiring process: Are you a good fit? What will it cost to hire you? These screening interviews typically last about 20 to 30 minutes and can cover a wide range of questions, including:

- ✓ Can you tell me about yourself?
- ✓ Why are you looking for a new opportunity?
- ✓ Why did you leave your previous company? (And sometimes the ones before that.)
- ✓ What are your salary expectations?
- ✓ What do you need to be successful?
- ✓ How would your supervisor (or previous supervisor) describe your work?
- ✓ Where do you need improvement?
- ✓ What's the accomplishment you're most proud of?

And while you're answering these and other questions, keep in mind you're being evaluated for:

- ✓ Education and training
- ✓ Work experience
- ✓ Skills (general and technical)
- ✓ Management experience if relevant
- ✓ Interpersonal skills
- ✓ Cultural fit
- ✓ Salary
- ✓ Personal attributes: enthusiasm, work ethic, honesty, and so on
- ✓ Overall competence as well as likeability

To make this even more complex, the HR interviewers can vary greatly in many aspects including age, style, experience, and preparedness. Some companies require in-depth interview training and provide specific guidelines and a list of core competencies for each position. Other companies offer no training and have a primitive method for evaluating candidates: thumbs up or thumbs down. Of course, you don't know, going into the interview, which situation you'll face, but it's often clear early on in the interview that you need to "run" the show or subtly guide the interviewer to the critical parts of your background that meet their needs. Let's look at sample answers to these typical questions and evaluate what makes the best answers.

Can you tell me about yourself?

You may be thinking: "Why are they asking me this when my resume is right in front of them?" Or you might wonder: "What kind of information do they want—where I was born, how many kids I have, my major in college?" *This seemingly innocent question is often a trap, so treat it seriously and be prepared. An HR executive I met with recently reminded me that often the HR interviewer hasn't read your resume, so you may be asked to go through your entire work history, starting with your first job and ending with the present.*

+A. I've always been interested in how things work, so after graduating from college with a degree in engineering, I worked for a year for a small firm here in Hartford. This gave me excellent exposure to the critical balance between engineering and business needs and I'm excited to bring that expertise to your firm. *This is a good answer because it's upbeat, logical, and shows why this person likes engineering.*

*A. I'm a mechanical engineer with the strong ability to create innovative solutions to practical problems. My work experience has given me the added perspective of understanding business needs, so unlike some engineers, I keep an eye on what the customer wants and our budget restraints while producing the best products. I'm confident I can do the same for your company. *This is a bit stronger, because it gives more details on what makes this person stand out as an engineer.*

!A. I'm a mechanical engineer with an advanced degree in engineering and experience working for a small engineering firm. What sets me apart from many in my field is that I have a strong drive to figure out how things work and then create cost-effective solutions. For example, when we didn't have the budget to buy the equipment we needed, I figured out a way to make it. Is this the kind of expertise you're looking for? *What makes this answer best is the specific example that proves the candidate's qualities and the use of a ZAP or probing question at the end. There is a slight risk that the HR interviewer may not want you to ask questions, and if that's the case, stop asking them.*

Every once in awhile the interviewer wants to know your personal background, not where you worked and your accomplishments. Here's a sample answer to that version of "Tell me about yourself." I grew up in Ohio just outside of Cleveland and was active in both sports and the drama club. After majoring in Engineering at RIT, I landed my first job with a small firm in the Detroit area. In my free time I coach soccer and also volunteer for Habitat for Humanity. These outside activities give me a chance to give back to my community and keep me energized and connected to others. *What this answer does not include is any religious, political, or highly personal information such as, "I just broke up with my boyfriend." It shows a highly motivated person who is more than his or her job.*

Why are you looking for a new opportunity?

The answer to this question depends on where you are in your career. If you're right out of high school or college, it's an easy answer: you're looking for your first job (although you may have worked while going to school). If, however, you've been working for 25 years, then this is what I typically call your "exit" statement, which zeroes in on why you were let go. Let's look at answers that address both ends of the spectrum.

+A. I'm excited to be looking for my first job in marketing. Although I did have an internship during college with a leading E-marketing firm, the position with your company would give me a broader background and would allow me to contribute in more areas. *This is upbeat and honest. This candidate can't "sell" in-depth experience because they don't have it. But the ending is good because it doesn't just talk about what the candidate will gain, but rather how those new skills and knowledge will help the company.*

I really enjoyed my 25 years with Zingo Marketing, but when they merged with Lakeside, many positions were eliminated, including mine. I'm excited to be looking for a new opportunity where I can use both my traditional marketing background and my cutting-edge knowledge of E-marketing to create winning campaigns. *In this instance, the candidate has to explain why he was let go and this example is good, because it's short and impersonal. It's also smart to quickly get to what you can do for the company and not dwell on the past.*

*A. I'm looking for a new opportunity because I just graduated from college with a degree in marketing. Two of my professors are willing to be references because they're confident I have a strong affinity for communicating value. One of my papers was published online, and in my two internships, I was exposed to various campaigns including one for food products and another for consumer goods. Because these are areas of interest to your firm, I believe this is a good match. *This is a better answer because it provides more details and makes use of references as a selling point.*

I really enjoyed my 25 years with Zingo Marketing, but when they merged with Lakeside, many positions were eliminated, including mine. If I understand the challenges facing your firm, you need to brand yourself as a leader in E-marketing so that you capture new clients while retaining your traditional accounts. At Zingo I did exactly that and won the President's Award for innovation. *This answer uses the same first sentence to quickly explain why the candidate is in the market. But then the candidate illustrates wonderful confidence in showing how he or she could help the company.*

!A. At Rutgers University where I graduated with honors in marketing, the curriculum was based on a balanced approach so that we were exposed to the real demands placed on marketing firms, as well as learning cutting-edge trends and technology. Having had several internships during college, I'm looking forward to joining a major firm like yours. *This gives more evidence of the candidate's value while still making it clear that this person is at the beginning of his or her career.*

I left Zingo Marketing after a highly successful career and I'm excited to use what I've learned to help another company become a leader in both traditional and E-marketing. If you take a look at my LinkedIn recommendations, you'll see that clients, peers, and vendors, as well as upper management, have recognized my broad abilities in creating winning marketing campaigns. For example, when Truvia was launched, I came up with an innovative five-part campaign that knocked the competition out of the water. I can give you details if you like, but with your track record in the food and consumer goods industries and my accomplishments, I know

I would be a strong addition to your firm. *In this version, the candidate skims over the exit statement and focuses quickly on the company at hand. Using LinkedIn as an outside resource is smart for two reasons: it provides credibility and shows that this person is with it despite a career of many years. Then they provide an example and tie it back to their value to the company.*

Why did you leave your previous company?

This is a variation of the previous question (Why are you looking for a new opportunity?). In some cases you could use the answers given for that question, but in others you may have to provide more reasons why your former company let you go. Typically the safe answers include: downsizings, mergers and acquisitions, plant closings, loss of sales or market share, and outsourcing.

+A. I left XYZ a month ago when they lost a major government contract. I learned a lot there and am excited to use my administrative skills with another leading defense organization. *This is a good answer because there are no red flags and nothing that might cause the interviewer to worry. And the candidate is positive about his or her former company—a critical part of your message in all interviews.*

*A. I would still be with XYZ, but unfortunately they lost a major government contract and my whole department was let go. I'm confident that I can apply what I learned in my five years there to your firm. If you talk to my references, they'll tell you I was the "go-to person." *This is a bit stronger because it makes it clear that the candidate enjoyed her previous job and by adding the references, she provides proof—or at least additional credibility—to her strong problem-solving skills.*

!A. I would still be with XYZ, but unfortunately they lost a major government contract and my whole department was let go. It was a great experience working there and it allowed me to support several different departments. From what I understand of your firm, you need an administrative assistant who can deal with multiple assignments simultaneously, who knows how to think and prioritize, and who doesn't leave until the job is done and done right. *Using the same beginning, this answer is more confident because the candidate clearly articulates her value. If she were unsure if she has hit the bull's-eye, she could then ask at the end, "Is that correct?"*

What are your salary expectations?

This is a dangerous question with a number of variations including "What were you making?" and "Can I see your most recent W-2?" The rule of thumb with salary or money conversations is that the first person to name a figure loses. So let's look at a few ways around this question as well as answers that won't hurt your chance of getting the compensation you want. A huge fear with this question is that if you ask for more money than the company intends to pay, you'll lose the offer. That is rarely the case unless you become inflexible or try to negotiate in too many other areas. (There's more information on how to negotiate in Chapter 26.)

+A. I'd be happy to share my salary requirements with you, but would you mind giving me your range for this position? I haven't worked for an architectural firm before, so I am not sure of your compensation guidelines. *This is a good ZAP—an attempt to get the person from the company—very often HR—to tell you their range. What makes this answer even better is that the candidate explains why they don't know what the compensation might be.*

*A. My salary expectations are flexible because right now I'm focusing on companies that are leaders in their field. If it's all right with you, I'd like to focus on the job itself first, and then discuss salary. Is that all right? *While being very polite, this answer postpones the salary talk—if the HR interviewer agrees to it. If you use this type of answer, be prepared for a "No." At that point you could use the answer in +A. or you might have to give a range, such as: "I'm looking for compensation in the 65 to low 70's range." Just be careful that you can* *live with the lower number because the HR interviewer may hold you to it.*

!A. I've been working for one firm for several years, and have just started looking for a new opportunity. I'm very happy to share my salary history with you, but I don't know yet how to answer your question. Do you have a range in mind? *This answer shows a high level of confidence and gives a credible reason for not answering the question while still demonstrating openness and trust.*

What do you need to be successful?

This is a somewhat vague question, which could be answered in several ways including the actual stuff you need (a computer, black-berry, company car, and so on) or the overall conditions that help you do your job well. If you're unsure of what the interviewer is asking, clarify this before you answer.

+A. In the three companies I've worked for throughout the past 15 years, I've learned that I do best when I have a support-ive boss and am part of a motivated team. I work very well inde-pendently, but enjoy the collaboration and creativity that comes from working with others. *What's good about this answer is that it's positive and focuses on ideal conditions and gives broad enough criteria that the candidate sounds reasonable and smart.*

*A. I've thought about this question quite a bit, as I've worked for large firms as well as start-ups, and have always managed a successful IT group. I like challenging situations—maybe it's a bit like having to get that paper written for college and it is 3 a.m. and your screen is still blank. Some people panic under pressure, but I love it. At the same time, I do well under more normal conditions. *In this answer, the candidate uses an analogy to help the interviewer understand how good he or she is under pressure. Because analogies paint pictures, they can be a powerful interview tool.*

!A. The three most critical things that lead to success are having a plan with a timeline, working in a collaborative environment where everyone helps each other, and gaining the trust of upper management. While at XYZ, it was precisely because of these three factors that I was able to reduce our manufacturing time from three days to just under a day, saving more than $5 million annually. Would you like me to go into more detail in terms of how I did this? *This answer is very strong because it's well organized and uses both an example and a ZAP to ensure that the interviewer is convinced. It also clearly shows that this candidate has thought about this issue and is well prepared.*

How would your supervisor (or former supervisor) describe your work?

This question gives you the chance to back up what you've said about yourself with evidence from others. Even if you're really not sure what he or she would say, you must come up with an answer that supports your key message about yourself—such as having good analytical skills or being a strong mentor for others. You can qualify the answer with a lead-in phrase such as "I'm pretty sure she would say..." or "Judging from my performance reviews, he would say..."

+A. My supervisor would say that I'm a hard worker and my track record shows that I always get the job done. *This is an okay answer, but doesn't offer enough proof or evidence to make it fully credible.*

*A. I was just rereading my performance appraisals and my most recent boss mentioned that I am the type of administrator who is self-motivated and who works well both individually and on teams. *This is a bit stronger because it uses the written words of the supervisor for the answer.*

!A. My past three supervisors all said the same thing to me: You're the kind of marketing manager who knows how to motivate a group and you have no hesitation in rolling up your sleeves and getting the job done. I recently was in charge of a campaign for a new, whitening toothpaste and we ran into several impasses with the agency we were using. When nothing seemed to work, I suggested we have lunch together to review the campaign and make sure we were hitting our target. This simple plan, which gave us time to talk through what needed to change, turned the project around and by the end of the first quarter, our sales exceeded our target. *This answer starts with a statement that clearly conveys the main selling point this candidate wants to communicate, and then uses an example or story to provide proof. Remember: Stories or examples are often what people remember—not generalizations.*

Where do you need improvement?

A variation on the weakness question, this one must be handled carefully because you never want to give an interviewer a reason not to hire you. At the same time, you have to show that you are human and have areas where you could do a bit better.

+A. In my role as a corporate trainer, I live and breathe presentations and my platform skills are excellent. Where I'd like to do better is in creating PowerPoint materials. I know how to use PowerPoint, but am not at the highest level. *If this candidate had reversed their answer and had admitted that their platform skills weren't the best, then they would have hurt themselves.*

*A. In my role as a corporate trainer, I live and breathe presentations and my platform skills are excellent. Where I'd like to do better is in creating PowerPoint materials, so I'm currently enrolled in a Skill Soft class to keep up with the latest features. *This is a better answer because the candidate is doing something about the weakness and therefore is illustrating that all-important quality—motivation.*

!A. As I look carefully at your job description, I don't see any obvious areas where my skills need improvement. But as an engineer with a passion for figuring out how things work, I'm always inventing the better mousetrap. In fact, I just had two patents approved. Do you have any particular questions about my background that I can answer? *An option in answering the weakness or improvement question is to say that you don't have any that would affect your ability to do this job. But you have to give the interviewer something. In this example, the candidate chose to ZAP to root out any concerns that might not have surfaced.*

What accomplishments are you most proud of?

When I ask my clients this, as part of interview preparation, I'm looking to see if they look and sound proud and excited, in addition to paying attention to the content of their answers. Remember: We believe what the body says more than we believe the words, so make sure your posture is good, that you're showing energy in your voice and gestures, and that your facial expression backs up your message.

+A. I'm really proud of the lesson plan I created to help fifth graders understand all the steps that go into writing a good report. Before this I had noticed how disorganized their research and writing were, and with my template the results were much better. *Giving before and after evidence, this is a fine answer although probably a bit short. Remember: The interviewer needs you to talk long enough to convince them and to give them a break before they have to ask another question.*

*A. I'm proud of the many ways I've contributed in my role as a career coach, but I guess I'm most proud of earning my CMF (Career Management Fellow) certification. I had hesitated to go for the top certification in our field, but with the support of an experienced sponsor, I broke the steps down into manageable pieces and got the work done. The final step—the interview—was a wonderful experience because it reinforced why I love this work: I get to be part of people's lives at a critical juncture and I'm always learning from my clients new ways to be successful in the job search. *Using somewhat informal language like "I guess," this answer* *tells a story starting with this candidate's fears, what she did to overcome them, and a strong result.*

!A. When I joined XYZ, the morale in the finance department was terrible. The former comptroller had created an atmosphere of mistrust, and as her replacement, I had to figure out how to turn that around. The first thing I did was to schedule individual meetings with everyone in the department—really just to listen to both what had happened and to find out what they needed. After that I put together a plan and included upbeat events such as a lunch and some team building exercises to help us meet our aggressive goals. Within six months there was a real transformation. As one manager told me, "I have to pinch myself when I come to work. It's a place of trust and collaboration and everything runs so smoothly." I know we have to be vigilant to maintain this culture, but I'm very proud of turning it around. *Great interview answers pull the interviewer into the candidate's world as this one does. We get to know this comptroller through this answer and gain the strong impression that here is a person who is unafraid to tackle tough problems.*

Ditch It

1. *Isn't that a question that the hiring manager should be asking?* It's not your role to question what the interviewer is asking and this negative question sets a combative tone.

2. *Can't we talk about salary later?* The intent here is good, but this is a rude way to defer naming your price.

3. *How do you know the needs of this department?* Although this could be a neutral question, it challenges the HR professional and could easily backfire.

4. *Can you tell me about the benefits?* It is not appropriate in a screening or HR interview to ask about the benefits. Only when you have an offer is it safe to ask this question.

Tips

✓ Do your best to get HR on your side. They're not the enemy and have in-depth knowledge of the company. Although an individual HR person's interview style might be formal and hard to read, try to establish rapport by listening carefully and playing by their rules.

✓ You are the expert on you and the HR recruiter has never done your job. Remember this should help you "sell" your skills with confidence. Tell yourself, just before the interview, "No one knows my brand better than me."

✓ Prepare specific questions that HR can answer. These could include asking about: the company culture, the hiring process, the job description, and other general information.

✓ Show that you've done your homework and are interested in this company for specific reasons. Needing a job is real, but that isn't what HR wants to hear.

✓ Respect the way the interview is run and the time table. For example, the HR interviewer may tell you that he or she is going to ask you seven questions, and that there will be time for your questions at the end. But, you may run out of time and never get to ask your questions. Don't let this throw you; you'll get to ask them at the next stage or you can put one or two in your follow-up or thank-you email.

✓ Make them like you. A senior HR client of mine got hired for a position that, in her words, "she wasn't qualified for". How did she do it? She made them (the interviewers, and in particular the hiring manager) like her by convincing them that she could do the job through careful listening and by using the company's mission statement in her answers.

13

RECRUITER INTERVIEWS

If I had a dollar for every job seeker I've worked with who complained about the way they were treated by recruiters, I'd be living on a tropical island. Why is this part of the job-search process fraught with such negative feelings? Because many job seekers don't understand the different types of recruiters and the way they work. Let's look at the types first:

Employment Agencies and Contract Firms

These are the companies that used to fill administrative and industrial jobs, but now also handle temporary positions of many levels. Some specialize in a particular industry such as pharmaceutical or clinical research, while others focus on specific functions such as IT, graphic design, or positions in finance. And some employment agencies or contract firms are "preferred vendors" meaning that a company uses them exclusively in hiring external candidates.

Contingency firms

These are the work horses of recruiters because most companies will give a listing for mid-management positions to more than one contingency firm. What this means is that these firms are competing with each other to get their candidate hired because their fees are contingent upon placement. So if XYZ needs a new Financial Analyst, they will give that posting to a number of contingency recruiters, but only pay the one who brings them the candidate they hire. This is where many job seekers get crazed, because they get a call from one of these firms, are told what a great match they are, and that they'll call them back the next day to arrange for an interview, and then they never hear from them again.

This is where we have what I call our "food chain" conversation: All recruiters work for themselves, for the companies that pay them, and then there's you. If you can keep in mind that you're third down on this chain, you'll be a lot less frustrated. As we look at how to handle recruiter interviews, please don't forget that many recruiters have excellent knowledge about resumes, an industry, specific companies, interviewing, and so on. My advice: learn how to work with them, because they can be a great help in your search.

Retained

These recruiters represent the high end of the spectrum and are retained by a company to fill executive-level positions. In other words, they handle exclusive assignments and are not competing with other firms. One retained recruiter who I interviewed didn't touch anyone whose compensation was under $250k. Another had clients who averaged closer to $350k. Retained recruiters have in-depth relationships with the companies they work with, have placed other candidates there so their knowledge is extensive and current, and are known for conducting extensive screening interviews that may include assessments. These recruiters work heavily on a referral basis (most effective when the referral is either from a candidate they've placed previously or from one of their client companies) and they don't have to place a high volume of candidates, because they receive about 30 to 35 percent of the candidate's yearly salary for handling most aspects of the search, including finding suitable candidates, screening them, checking their references, preparing them for the interviews, administering assessments if required, negotiating, and even helping with on-boarding. And sometimes their searches are highly confidential as when they're replacing a CEO, so discretion is another key requirement.

One retained recruiter I spoke with told me that his client companies pressure him not to submit candidates who are in transition. He can, of course, include an executive who is in transition along with other candidates, but because these are top executive positions, the expectation is that many of them are working. Fit is a critical issue with retained recruiters and there are various ways they determine this starting with the candidate's resume, then a half hour phone screen that focuses on that person's work history, followed by an in-person interview with the recruiter (usually several hours long) that is behavioral based and might include questions such as, "What were you hired to do? What problems did you inherit and how did you deal with them? How were you successful in overcoming resistance? How would your biggest adversary describe you?" The top candidates who make it past this stage are then interviewed by the company and, if selected, may then have to undergo assessments to dig deeper into their leadership personality and abilities. (A few firms that offer these are TAI, Inc., ghSMART, Gallup, and RHR International.) The retained recruiter prepares the candidate for these steps and also handles most, if not all of the negotiations once an offer has been made.

Why would you want to add recruiters to the ways you're looking for a new position? The simple answer is that they have relationships with companies that you don't and therefore could make your search easier and shorter. Another answer is that you can learn from them. And lastly, if you can develop a good, working relationship with recruiters, you now have made an investment in your career. In other words, it's smart to make recruiters part of your career care and maintenance even if you're happily employed. Many clients of mine have landed wonderful jobs because they had stayed in touch with recruiters and had helped them by referring other candidates to them. (This, by the way, is a really smart thing to do. If you get a call from a recruiter and the position isn't a fit, see if you can refer them to someone you know who would be better for the job. The recruiter won't forget you.)

One last thing before we look at what to expect from interviews with recruiters: If you want to work sooner rather than later, be open to contract or temporary work. (This rarely applies to executive positions.) My most unpopular phrase as a career coach is "All jobs are temporary," because from my perspective they are. This doesn't mean disregard the difference between being hired and gaining all kinds of benefits including medical, a 401(k), bonuses, training, and so on, but it does mean don't create such a huge barrier in your mind that you dismiss this kind of work. It's not uncommon for temp positions to become permanent, and nothing says you can't continue your search while working. Also, don't be offended if one of the first questions you're asked is about compensation. Recruiters and agencies have to find candidates who will work for what their client companies pay. As we look at sample questions and answers, you'll see how to handle the money question.

Employment Agencies and Contract Firms

Lois is an Administrative Assistant who sent her resume to 10 local agencies that are strong in the administrative field, followed up with phone calls, and was scheduled for an in-person screening interview.

Thanks, Lois, for coming in today. Can you tell me why you're looking for a new position?

+A. Certainly. My last position was a contract one and once the work was done, I was let go. *This is not a great answer because it's too short and doesn't make Lois sound either valuable or motivated.*

*A. Yes, I'd be glad to. I was hired by Novartis on a contract basis as the Administrative Assistant was out on maternity leave. Once she came back, I was no longer needed. *This is a bit better as the interviewer has more information, but again it's too short and doesn't "sell" Lois effectively.*

!A. Yes, I'd be glad to. I was hired by Novartis on a contract basis as the Administrative Assistant was out on maternity leave. It was a wonderful opportunity to support several team leaders and to schedule all their meetings and travel arrangements. I have excellent references from these team leaders that I'd be glad to share with you, and I'm excited to be looking for a new opportunity where I can use my organizational skills and ability to multitask to help another organization. *Here, Lois gives the interviewer real substance and comes across as motivated and upbeat. She also ties what she has just done at her last assignment to what she can do for the next place she works. This is a great selling point.*

Note: With administrative positions there are often tests to check the candidate's expertise with Microsoft Office or expense or scheduling software. The worst story I have heard about one of these exams was a job seeker who was put in a room and given 15 minutes to complete an assessment. An hour later she finally came out of the room and walked back to the front desk in the office on her own, because they had forgotten about her!

Lois, can you please tell me what kind of compensation you're looking for?

+A. Well, I can tell you what I was making. *Although including past compensation isn't a bad idea, this answer is too short and doesn't give the agency the information they need.*

*A. I'd be glad to. As my last two assignments were a bit different, let me tell you about both. I earned $20 an hour with no overtime at XYZ, and with my most recent company, I made $18 an hour with overtime and paid holidays. *This is better because Lois gives the interviewer specific compensation information.*

!A. I'd be happy to. Could I ask you first, what kind of range you have in mind for this position? Let's say the interviewer says, "We were thinking of $18 to 22 an hour." Then Lois would say: Something toward the top of that range would be fine. I was earning $20 an hour with no overtime at XYZ, and with my most recent company, I made $18 an hour with overtime and paid holidays. *This answer reinforces the bedrock rule of negotiating: The one who mentions the exact amount first, loses. But notice that Lois still shares her salary information. Be prepared with agencies and contract work for very little salary flexibility. They often have set rates and have to add their fees to what you're making. I tell my clients to look at the overall package—not just the compensation. But if the pay is really low and you have to drive an hour and a half to get to work in terrible traffic and you won't be gaining any new skills or industry contacts, then it may not be worth it.*

Why would you be interested in contract work, Peter, after being an employee for the past 15 years?

+A. It was wonderful being with XYZ for a long stretch, but I figure contract work will help me understand the way other companies do business and will give me a better idea of what I'd like to do next. *Although Peter's reasons for being interested in contract work aren't bad, this answer makes him sound unsure of his plans and could make the interviewer feel that he's unlikely to stay in the job.*

*A. I'm very excited about contract work as it gets me using my strong finance skills quickly. And although I'm up-to-date in my field, I recognize that working for a new company will broaden my knowledge. *This answer is upbeat and a bit more specific, but keeps the focus on Peter—never the best way to prove value.*

!A. While working at XYZ, I never thought about contract work, but as I've learned about opportunities through your firm, I realize it's an exciting way for a win-win: I get back to work quickly and the company gets a CPA with broad experience. Also, at this point in my career, I'm open to short-term assignments, so I can be flexible and go where the need is. *Here, Peter shows what he's learned about contract work, and he balances the benefit for himself with the value he would bring to the company.*

Applications and Forms

Employment agencies and contract firms often have you fill out applications. Here's a list of what might be included:

- ✓ Name, address, phone.
- ✓ Social Security Number.
- ✓ Position you're applying for and the date.
- ✓ How many hours you can work and whether you're seeking full-time or part-time work.
- ✓ Education (high school, college, trade or professional school, advanced degrees).
- ✓ Criminal history—if you've been convicted of a crime, and if so, space to explain.
- ✓ Whether you're legally eligible for employment in this country.
- ✓ Driver's license—if you have one and the number on your license.
- ✓ Military background—if you've served and if you're now in the National Guard or Military Reserves.

✓ Work history starting with the most recent and then either going back a specific number of years, or a specific number of employers; a short description of your work and the name of your supervisor and his or her title, as well as your title; and addresses and phone numbers are often requested.

✓ Salary history. What you earned most recently as well as in earlier jobs.

✓ Permission to contact your present or past employers.

✓ References with phone numbers, emails, and sometimes how they know you.

✓ Signature and date.

Two additional resources for helping you with job applications are *www.Quintessentialcareers.com* and "Introduction to Job Applications" by J. Michael Farr and Susan Christophersen.

Contingency Recruiters

Hi, Bob. This is Simon calling from Get-the-Job Recruiters. We're looking for an IT Manager who is up-to-date in technology and also able to manage people for a position we're filling at a local financial services firm. Can you tell me if this sounds like you?

+A. Sure. Just to back up, how did you find my resume? (Simon tells him he found it on Monster.) Yes, I'm current with the latest applications and, although I didn't have a staff, I led a team of other programmers. *It probably doesn't matter how the recruiter found you, so if that's a question you want to ask, it would be better to hold it for later on in the interview. This question is a specific version of the "tell me about yourself" question, and Bob's answer is weak because it's too short and a bit general.*

*A. Yes, it does. I've been in IT my whole career and pride myself in staying up-to-date in the field. In fact, in the past year I've been teaching an online college course that has kept my skills sharp. I also enjoy managing people and am known as a good motivator. My team appreciates the fact that I'm not removed from them and that I can help them solve technical problems. *A better answer, Bob addresses the two parts of the question, but his example (teaching an online college course) may or may not convince Simon that he will be a good match for the job.*

!A. Certainly. And thanks for calling. One of my trademarks is staying current with technology, which as you know, changes very quickly. I'm up-to-date with cloud computing and am active in a professional association where we keep track of trends for mobile devices. In my last position, I managed a group of 15 programmers and found that my combination of technical know-how and my people skills made me highly effective. In fact, I was voted best manager of the year my last two years. Does that give you enough detail? *This answer, with a ZAP at the end, is the best because Bob gives evidence of both his technical and managerial skills. Notice how Bob also sets a polite and professional tone right at the start by thanking the recruiter for calling. Courtesy works!*

Hi Sue, I found your resume on Indeed and you look like a great match for an HR position I'm filling. Are you still with XYZ?

+A. No, I'm not. My job was eliminated last month and I'm actively looking for new HR opportunities. *Sue's answer is weak as she misses the chance to talk about the "great match," and gives a short and vague response, which does not make her sound either strong or motivated.*

*A. Thanks for calling. I'm sorry, I didn't catch your name. (The recruiter says her name is Nancy.) What happened at XYZ, Nancy, is that we bought another company and as a result of the integration, many positions were cut, including mine. Could you tell me more about the position you're filling? *This is much stronger because*

Sue gets and uses the recruiter's name and then quickly goes through her exit or why-I'm-no-longer-with-the-company statement and asks a question to get the focus on the match.

A! I appreciate your call. May I ask your name? (The recruiter says her name is Nancy.) I'm no longer with XYZ, Nancy, and am excited about finding a new position in which I can use my broad, generalist skills to help another company build and maintain an excellent HR department. *In this answer, Sue decides not to go into the reasons she was let go, but instead puts the emphasis on who she is and what she has to offer, reinforcing the "great match" concept.* (Note: Sue's resume might have "present" written for her most recent company dates so that the reader doesn't know if she is still working there are or not. Many job seekers do this while they're receiving severance and some do it beyond that date to avoid being discriminated against for being unemployed.)

Joe, I've got a six-month contract for someone with an operations background like yours. Can you start right away?

+A. Thanks for calling. My schedule is flexible, but could you please tell me more about the position? *Not a bad answer, this tells the recruiter that Joe can work right away, but doesn't reinforce his operations background.*

*A. Nice to hear from you. I'm open to contract work and can start when needed. With 20 years in operations in both publishing and manufacturing, I'm excited to be looking for new opportunities where I can improve efficiency and cut costs as I have throughout my career. Could you please tell me a bit more about what this company is looking for? *Even though Joe doesn't have any information about this contract, he includes a generic pitch. Because contingency recruiters work very quickly, this is a smart strategy as Joe has begun to prove his value before he asks for more information.*

!A. Thanks for calling me. I'm open to contract work and can start when needed. What distinguishes my work in operations is my ability to work with employees of all levels to run the best plant possible, always meeting deadlines and keeping costs under budget. Would you mind telling me a bit more about what you're looking for? *The reason this answer is a bit stronger than the previous one is it focuses on Joe's competitive advantage in operations, rather than on industries. When you're giving an answer and you don't know the industry, it's safer to stay with your basic skills and value. And by being specific, he has given the recruiter both a reason to select him and information that he—the recruiter—can share with the hiring company.*

Retained Recruiters

Thanks, Cheryl, for telling me about your background. I see you majored in biology in college. Why was that? (This question would be part of the recruiter's initial phone interview.)

+A. I was good in science in high school and thought I might want to be a doctor, so biology made sense. *A weak answer, Cheryl doesn't help the recruiter to get to know her. Remember: This person plays a critical role in determining if you will be selected for the interviews with the company, and as one recruiter told me, "As I listen to answers, I want the candidate to fail so that I can shorten my list."*

*A. I fell in love with biology in high school and continued to be passionate about it in college. I wasn't sure what my profession would be until I had an internship with a small medical device firm in my junior year. That's when I realized I had a good head for business and changed my major. And that eventually led me to becoming the CFO for a firm that makes artificial skin. *This answer almost makes it because Cheryl shows a passion for biology and explains how she ended up in business.*

!A. I fell in love with biology in high school and continued to be passionate about it in college. I wasn't sure what my profession would be until I had an internship with a small medical device firm in my junior year. That's when I realized I had a good head for business and changed my major. And that eventually led me to becoming the CFO for a firm that makes artificial skin. My educational background in biology has served me in many ways and allows me to understand our products and the work that goes into developing them, on a much deeper basis. *Using the same beginning, this answer is stronger as it connects Cheryl's past with her present situation and includes a strong selling point.*

As you know, Cheryl, we're filling a CFO position at a leading cosmetics firm, and this is highly confidential as the current CFO is still in place. Could you give me a specific example of how you've handled highly sensitive issues in the past? (This question would probably be in the face-to-face interview with the retained recruiter and Cheryl may not yet know the name of the company filling the position.)

+A. Certainly, Greg. Having worked in finance for many years, when I became Director of Finance for XYZ, we had an unusual situation. The person I reported to was involved in practices that raised some questions, and I was asked by the CEO, as this was a small firm, to document the information that my boss gave me. I had a good relationship with this person, but understood that our company ethics came first. To this day, my boss doesn't know that I was part of the investigation. *Cheryl's answer shows she can handle confidentiality, but it doesn't position her as CFO material.*

*A. Yes, Greg, I would be glad to. With an MBA in finance and in-depth experience making high-level financial decisions, I've learned how to balance a company's mission and ethics with practical steps that must be taken to keep the business successful. At my most recent company, I was part of a committee that reviewed some financial irregularities that were troubling. I'm not at liberty to give you details, but I'm happy to tell you that we conducted this investigation with 100 percent confidentiality and in the end discovered that the problem was not misconduct, but rather was caused by a system error. That kind of trust is one of my trademarks. *This is a much stronger answer because Cheryl demonstrates confidentiality while using her answer to position herself as a financial leader.*

!A. Yes, I can, Greg. In my experience, having held senior finance positions with Fortune 100 companies, confidentiality and trust are core issues that are often difficult to determine from someone's resume. I will give you several examples in which my ability to keep important information confidential was critical. I was promoted to Director of Finance because, although we were negotiating a highly sensitive acquisition, only the CEO and a few other key players knew about it. It was my negotiating skills combined with my airtight confidentiality that made this work. Another time, we were worried about negative media coverage on a highly sensitive issue that could have damaged our company's reputation. I not only spearheaded our successful strategy for turning this around, but also trained the entire finance department so that each person knew what to do if approached by the media. If considered for this CFO position, any information you share with me will go no further. *What puts this answer over the top is the effective set-up at the start—positioning confidentiality and trust as paramount to success—and then two specific examples that prove that Cheryl practices what she preaches. Notice the effective tie-back at the end—she connects her answer to the CFO position.*

Although you would be part of the C-Suite here, the parent company located in Europe has final control. How would you resolve differences with them?

+A. I'm a consensus seeker so I'd find out their concerns, discuss the pros and cons with my team, and reach a workable compromise. *This is not a C-Suite or executive answer. Although building consensus isn't a bad idea, the candidate doesn't come across as a decisive leader who could deal effectively with conflict.*

*A. I always think it's a good idea to get to know people. As part of the on-boarding process, I'd want to spend some time in Europe so that those folks would know me and I them. That way, when things heat up, we'll know how to deal with each other. As COO (Chief Operations Officer) I know what I have to do, and if they come up with ideas that I know won't fly, I'll explain that to them, but at the end of the day, I've got to do what's right for the company. *Another nonexecutive answer, this one is full of land mines. The language is way too informal and the candidate ends up sounding bullheaded and difficult. A retained recruiter would most likely never let someone who talks like this anywhere near the hiring company.*

!A. When I consider differences of opinion—and in this case with the parent company—I first want to understand the background. As the new COO I would make sure I was up-to-speed on what has happened throughout the past few years and I'd make a point to get different opinions. Next, because one of my trademarks is transparency, I'd do my best to create clear communications with our parent company and spend time in Europe, if that's practical. Before launching any new initiatives, I'd ensure that the parent company understands them in detail and sees the value. And lastly, because I firmly believe that most ideas end up better when diverse opinions are sought out, I'd work hard to make sure our lines of communication stay open. Let me give you a quick example of how I resolved a similar conflict a few years ago. (For the sake of space I'm omitting the example, but note the tie back that would follow it.) This shows that I'm a skilled listener and negotiator and know how to work effectively with all parties. *Here, we see an answer that a retained recruiter would expect. The candidate shows tremendous confidence as he or she provides a step-by-step approach that includes selling points. And while length isn't everything, answers must do a job; in this case it must prove that the candidate can succeed in a complicated reporting structure. By helping the recruiter understand what he or she would do and by using an example and tie-back, this answer provides evidence that this person could do the job and do it well.*

Ditch It!

1. *Can't we talk about compensation after I know more about the job?* Although this is often a good idea, it probably won't work with recruiters. They have to know if you're going to fit within the range the company has given them.

2. *What's wrong with you people? You keep calling me for jobs in IT and I'm not a programmer.* Yes, it's very possible that a recruiter looks at your resume quickly and makes a mistake. It would be better to see if you need to tweak your resume or if they have a division that works more closely with your background.

3. *I don't want to go on the interview. It's too long of a commute.* Only you can decide what kind of commute is going to work for you, but don't use this excuse with recruiters because they won't call you again. My general advice is to go on interviews unless you're going to be at a serious disadvantage, meaning you really don't have the skills the company wants. Location is one of the most slippery parts of interviewing and you don't want to miss out on opportunities that have a work-from-home policy, or a branch that's closer to you, or the chance to get introduced to one of their partners who could be a critical part of your network.

4. *I can't talk right now—I'm late for a meeting. Can we talk next week?* Your job is to make things easy for the recruiter. Although you may have to run to a meeting, don't ask him or her to wait a week.

5. *Can I follow up with you in a few days?* What recruiters will accept or tolerate in terms of follow-up will vary extensively, but it's best to ask the recruiter what is appropriate. One retained recruiter I spoke with suggested every six weeks for general follow-up. When a search is active, of course, you'll be in contact much more frequently.

Tips

- ✓ Never pay money to a recruiter. Their fees are paid by the company with the open position—not by you. If you get a call from a recruiter who requests payment, politely tell them that this is not the way recruiters work and that you're not interested.
- ✓ Cultivate relationships with recruiters and employment agencies—it's a smart part of the care and maintenance of your career.
- ✓ Ask coworkers or former coworkers if they are willing to share their recruiter contacts with you.
- ✓ Go for volume and you'll get to quality. Don't send your resume to three recruiters or agencies and think you've done a good job. You need to reach out to 10, 20, or 30 or more. Think of this as casting a wide net. Then see what you catch.
- ✓ Be nice to recruiters even when their demands frustrate you. By remembering where you are in the food chain, this becomes much easier.
- ✓ Consider contract work as a way to get in the door with a company, and don't forget, many companies use this as a first step. Once they see the work you can do, you could be hired on a "permanent" basis. Even if the work is contract only, you're working again, you have new people in your network, and won't have as big a gap on your resume.
- ✓ Don't cheat on your preparation, especially with retained recruiters. Most are skilled interviewers and they'll dig down to see if you really can do the things your resume says you can.
- ✓ Do everything you can to prove that you're a good fit for the position—not just in terms of the day-to-day work, but also culturally. Poor fit is one of the biggest reasons recruiters reject candidates.

14

BEHAVIORAL: LET ME SEE YOU IN ACTION

This common type of interview is a challenge for many job seekers because they aren't prepared for the level of detail the interviewer requires. What is a behavioral interview and what is its purpose? Typically, this type of interview drills down into the specifics of what you did in a particular situation. Often starting with phrases such as "Tell me about a time" or "Describe how you handled," the interviewer wants to see, step-by-step, how you solved a problem or handled a difficult situation. The theory behind this type of interview is that past behavior is an accurate predictor of future behavior—in other words, if interviewers get a clear sense of what you did in a former job, this will give them an accurate picture of what you'd be like to work with now.

Let's look at the best ways to prepare for this type of interview and then go through some questions and answers. Many job seekers avoid the necessary preparation for behavioral interviews because it's a lot of work, but try to look at it this way: If you can do well in behavioral interviews, you're probably going to have an easy time with more general questions. Here's what you need to be ready:

- ✓ Examine the job description and break it down into specific skills or requirements (see the MAP in Chapter 1).
- ✓ Create accomplishment stories (Chapter 2) for each skill or requirement.
- ✓ Review past performance reviews, awards, LinkedIn recommendations, and whatever other materials you have that relate to your past work.
- ✓ Organize your accomplishment stories by categories such as: problem-solving, analytical skills, situations that you couldn't control, difficulty with a boss and/ or subordinate, weakness, what others say about you, and so on.
- ✓ Make sure that you include details in your sample stories: You must be able to walk the interviewer through exactly what you did (and in some cases your thinking process) for each step.
- ✓ Create a list of the behaviors you want to highlight. There are many of these, but your list could include: decisiveness, energy, insight, taking initiative, leadership, mentoring, planning, and so on.
- ✓ Think of big concepts instead of memorizing answers to a long list of questions. When you're nervous, memorized answers will disappear on you, but preparing good specific answers to the categories listed in the previous bullet will give you a strong foundation and will be easier to remember.

Harry, could you please tell me about a time when you were unable to complete a project on time and how you handled it?

This question focuses on time management but also communication skills, as the interviewer is curious to see how Harry behaved in a tight spot. This reveals more about Harry then when things were going smoothly, so it's a test of character as well.

+A. I can't think of a time when that happened because of my efforts, but I can tell you about a situation when we didn't meet a key deadline because our new manufacturer messed up. When I was with Widget, Inc., we won a large contract for our packaging materials, but at the same time we had just outsourced our manufacturing to India. I was against it, but no one listened to me. So when the order didn't arrive on time, I told my boss that this is what you get when you try to cut costs. It was an unfortunate situation. *This is a weak answer, because Harry sounds defensive, he blames others, and his tone is much too informal. It's not professional to use language like "messed up" or "no one listened to me."*

*A. Sure, I'd be happy to. When I was with Widget, Inc., we won a large contract for our packaging materials, but at the same time we had just outsourced our manufacturing to India. Unfortunately, we agreed to an aggressive date to have the packaging ready, and ended up having to explain to the client why they didn't receive their order until three weeks late. When we looked at it carefully, we realized that there were too many parts of the process we couldn't control given that this was a new situation. After this happened, I sat down with my boss to see if we could devise a way to avoid these problems. He appreciated my efforts, and in the future we were able to predict our turnaround time much more accurately. *This is a better answer because it reveals the steps Harry took to solve a difficult situation and he shows his problem-solving abilities and that he's proactive. But it doesn't address the "elephant in the room"—what happened with the client?*

!A. Sure, I'd be happy to. When I was with Widget, Inc., we won a large contract for our packaging materials, but at the same time we had just outsourced our manufacturing to India. Upper management thought they were agreeing to a reasonable delivery date, but in one of our staff meetings before the contract was signed, I raised questions about how predictable our new manufacturer was. Unfortunately, we agreed to an aggressive date to have the packaging ready, and ended up having to explain why the client didn't receive the order until three weeks after it was due. Because I was the project lead, I asked if we could offer the client a discount on their next order to offset their frustration with our late delivery. This was accepted and saved us from losing a key client. I also put practices in place that would prevent this type of problem from happening again. *This is the best answer, because Harry clearly shows the steps he took and even that he was concerned about predicting how quickly the new manufacturer would be able to produce the materials. It also shows creativity, because Harry came up with a solution that helped retain a key client and prevent future problems.*

Selena, can you describe how you handled a disagreement with your boss?

This is one of those questions that backs you into a corner. What if you never experienced this, or what if you did, but would rather not talk about it? With practice, even this challenging behavioral question can be answered safely.

+A. I can't think of a time when I had a disagreement with my boss as I very rarely see her. She works out of our Colorado office and I'm here in Indiana. Mostly she sends me emails and outlines what she wants me to get done. That has never caused a problem. *This answer doesn't give the interviewer what he or she wants, and although it may be truthful, it needs to address the "conflict" issue.*

*A. When I started my career in publishing, I had a wonderful boss who helped me understand the critical issues in becoming a successful publicist. One time he told me that the campaign I was working on was too narrow and that I wasn't reaching key targets. I didn't agree as I was confident that the campaign would work more effectively from the ground up. After thinking about his comments for a few days, I asked for time to talk and we went over the strategy together. In the end, we were both right—what I was doing was effective, but there were some issues that he understood better than I did. The result was a highly successful campaign that helped one of our authors gain national media attention. *This is a much better answer because it provides details and shows great confidence. For Selena to have the courage to "disagree" with her boss shows a person with both independence and integrity. Also, she's a big enough person to admit that she learned from her boss.*

!A. Just two months after I was hired, my boss told me that she had hired me because I was the kind of person who stands up for what she believes. Many of the other candidates struck her as soft—people who would agree to anything just to get the job. The test of this came a bit later when she asked me to write a report about our most recent experience with a particular client. I had been involved with this author from the start, and knew that he was often unreasonable and demanding. To make matters worse, he never met his deadlines. When I submitted a draft of this report to my boss, she told me to rewrite it because it was "way too negative." I worked on it for a few days and sent her an updated draft. She still didn't like it. I then asked if we could schedule a brief meeting because I needed help in understanding the purpose of the report. Once that happened, I was able to find the correct middle ground—a report that was both diplomatic and accurate. It was a great learning experience. *This answer turns a potential weakness into a strength by showing that independent thinking is one of Selena's key attributes while also illustrating her willingness to compromise and learn.*

Bob, can you please tell me about a time when you had to make a difficult decision?

Here the interviewer wants to get inside your brain and find out how you think under pressure. The tough situations that we have to resolve, of course, say more about who we are than the easy ones. So although this is a tricky question to answer, it provides a strong platform for selling your top skills (critical thinking, problem-solving, creativity, collaboration, and so on.)

+A. Well, I guess this is an example. I had two deadlines at once—one from my boss and one from her boss. I really didn't know what to do so I tried to meet both by staying late and working over the weekends. But then it dawned on me that I wasn't getting paid for all this extra work, so I finished the project for my boss and figured she would explain the situation to her boss. The rest is history. I never knew exactly what happened, but I think not meeting that deadline kept me from being promoted. *This answer creates serious problems for Bob. Using informal language like "I guess" makes a weak beginning and what we learn about Bob is that he resented the extra work so he ignored a critical deadline. This shows poor communication and problem-solving skills, and at the end, he sounds as if he feels sorry for himself for not getting a promotion. Not so good!*

* A. Yes. When I landed my first job out of college as a programmer with AT&T, we were asked to completely revise a system that had many bugs. I was too new to question whether we had the resources to fix this system, but it soon became obvious to me and the rest of the team that we were going to fail. We would fix one part of the program and that would cause problems in another area. We just couldn't get our heads above water. My boss called a meeting and together we came up with several steps—including getting some outside help—that allowed us to not only fix the errors with the current system, but also prevent future glitches. It was a great experience for me because I learned how important it is to analyze problems carefully up front and to make sure we have the right tools to fix them. *This is a good answer because Bob is specific—he lets us know where he was working and when, as well as the particulars of the situation. By giving credit to his boss and the team, he proves that he works well with others. And he ends by calling this a "great experience"—a positive way to wrap up his difficult decision.*

!A. When I landed my first job out of college as a programmer with AT&T, we were asked to completely revise a system that had many bugs. I was too new to question whether we had the resources to fix this system, but it soon became obvious to me and the rest of the team that we were going to fail. We would fix one part of the program and that would cause problems in another area. We just couldn't get our heads above water. I asked my boss if we could schedule a meeting to look at this situation together, and he not only agreed, but he asked me to run the meeting. I spoke individually with each member of the team before the meeting so that I had a clear outline of the problems we were experiencing as well as some possible solutions. The meeting was great! Within an hour we had a clear plan of action that our boss then took to senior management. Once we got approval—and part of our solution was getting outside resources—we were able to move ahead effectively and fix both current and future problems. It was a good lesson in how important it is to be proactive when faced with a challenge, and I learned to look carefully at our resources when agreeing to project deadlines. *Using the same beginning, Bob's answer here is the best because he shows initiative and gives more details about how he turned a difficult situation into a success.*

Sylvia, could you please tell me about a situation where you were misunderstood by others in your office?

This question is a fishing expedition to find out if you're difficult to get along with and tend to blame others for misunderstandings. Let's look at answers that address this directly, as well as one that tells the interviewer this hasn't happened.

+A. I'd be happy to, Sue, but looking back over my career as a Customer Service Rep, I really can't think of a time when that happened. I can, however, give you an example from the professional association I attend. A few years ago I was Chair of the new member committee for Customer Service International, and I thought we should create a welcome packet for new members. Another woman on the committee disagreed with me and was certain that this was a waste of money. I tried explaining the bene-fits of making people feel welcome at our meetings, but she stone-walled every suggestion I had. I then scheduled time to talk with her privately, but that didn't help. When it came to a vote, I had enough support to get the resolution through, but she was so upset that she quit and never came back. *It's okay that Sylvia states that she hasn't experienced this situation at work, but her example from her association is fraught with problems. Although she looks like an effective communicator, she comes across as stubborn and determined to get her own way. Also, the ending is negative and it leaves a bad impression.*

*A. Sure, Sue. I'd be happy to. In the second marketing firm I worked for—which was a small company—the support staff was used to a slow pace, and as my friends say "I have two speeds, fast and faster." So without my realizing it, they felt threatened by my pace and thought I was judging theirs, which I wasn't. When one admin came into my office and yelled at me, I realized I had to do something. So once I calmed down, I made a real effort to slow down, while still getting my work done. I suggested we eat lunch together once or twice a week, and I was more careful not to ex-pect a quick turnaround on the work I gave them. This turned the misunderstanding around, and we worked together much more smoothly. *This is better than the previous answer in that Sylvia gives a good example of being misunderstood, but it's a high-risk answer be-cause she comes across as somewhat arrogant and also doesn't really solve the critical issue of how work gets done in the office.*

A! Yes, Sue, I can. In the second marketing firm I worked for—which was a small company—I made the mistake of assum-ing that the culture of the office was similar to my last position with a large firm. It took me a few months to realize that the pace was much slower and that the support staff—who were long-term employees and were used to this pace—perceived me as arrogant because my way of doing things was much faster. Once I recog-nized the problem, I slowed down and also made a concerted effort to speak frequently with the support staff. It took a little time, but by my six-month mark, the misunderstanding had turned into real collaboration and respect for each other, which of course meant that we were meeting our deadlines. It was a good lesson for me to learn and I've made sure to remember it, especially when starting with a new company. *This is the best answer because Sylvia admits, right up front, that she made a mistake. She then explains why that happened as well as the steps she took to resolve the misunderstanding. And she then ties the results back to work—to productivity—which broadens her answer and allows her to sell her effectiveness.*

George, can you please tell me about a time you persuaded someone you worked with that your plan was the way to go and how you did that?

Here, the focus is communication skills mixed with personality. How you change someone's mind is a powerful way to find out how you interact with others, as well as how you deal with potential conflict. If you can't think of an example from your work history (or if you're applying for your first job), then pick something from school, an internship, or volunteering—just be careful to stay clear of religion and politics.

+A. Let me think for a minute. As you know, I graduated from college a few months ago, so I don't have a lot of work experience. But when I was a lifeguard at the Parkside Country Club, I noticed that many of the lifeguards got bored and didn't watch the swimmers as carefully as they should. I asked the pool manager if I could bring up a suggestion at our weekly staff meeting and he agreed. What I suggested was a better rotation of posts so that each guard moved from the baby pool to the mid-sized pool and then on to the one with lap lanes. Several of the lifeguards who had worked there for years didn't like the suggestion, because they had their favorite spots that were near the office where they kept their drinks and snacks. I outlined the benefits of the new rotation and suggested we try it for a week or two and then have a vote on it. The manager agreed and I got enough votes that the policy was put in place. *This isn't a great answer, because it starts off admitting to lack of experience and doesn't show that George persuaded the long-term life guards. In fact, a hiring manager could come to the conclusion that he forced them into a change of policy that they disliked, and therefore that he could create conflict in his next job.*

*A. Yes, I can. When I was a lifeguard at the Parkside Country Club, I noticed that many of the life guards got bored and didn't watch the swimmers as carefully as they should. As I thought about it I realized that it was hard to stay focused when sitting in the hot sun for hours. We all did what we could to stay sharp and keep the clients safe, but I got the idea that if we had more variety in our daily routine, we'd all do better. So I made a presentation at our weekly staff meeting that changed our times in the chair from 45 minutes to 30 minutes and that varied our duties during each shift. When I saw that some of the long-term life guards resisted these ideas, I asked them for theirs. This created an open discussion and the end results were a good compromise that we all agreed would work. *This is a better answer because we see George in action and get a sense of his communication and negotiating skills. The ending is a bit weak because it doesn't tie back to the critical point of the question: persuasion.*

!A. Yes, I'd be happy to. When I was a lifeguard at the Parkside Country Club, I noticed that many of the lifeguards got bored and didn't watch the swimmers as carefully as they should. I realized I didn't know why this was happening, so during our breaks, I took an informal survey and asked the other lifeguards if there were changes to our schedules that could make us better at our jobs. The one issue that I heard over and over again was how hard it was to focus when there was so little change during the day. I then asked our boss, the pool manager, if I could have five minutes at our next staff meeting and he agreed. I outlined a schedule rotation that would give each of us much more variety, including the other tasks we were responsible for, such as moving lounge chairs, cleaning bathrooms, and so on. When the manager asked for a vote it was unanimous, because everyone had been instrumental in the suggestions. I learned a great lesson from this about getting early buy-in and was really proud of making our pool a safer place for the club members. *This is a wonderful answer from someone early in his career. George answers the question with excellent specifics and proves that he is a great team player who takes pride in his work.*

Gladys, tell me what kind of leader you are and give me an example that proves your leadership strengths.

This two-part question offers the job candidate—you—a great chance to sell yourself. The first part asks for descriptors (which are easy because no one is going to describe his leadership style as faltering, weak, or dictatorial), but the second half, as is true of all behavioral questions, requires specific proof. It is these details that will either convince the interviewer or not. A quick note on multiple part questions: Make it the interviewer's job to remember the parts, not yours. If, under stress, you forget the second part of question, you can politely ask, "Could you please repeat the second part of the question?"

+A. If you take a look at my performance reviews throughout the past 15 years, you'll see one phrase over and over: strong leader with the ability to work well with all levels of staff. I pride myself on an open-door policy, so if the hourly workers have a problem, they know they can walk in my office. But I'm just as effective with upper management. I know they don't have much time, so I distill my presentations and reports for them down to the essence of what they need to know. *Gladys starts out with a strong first sentence, but then gets bogged down in details that are relevant but don't provide enough proof of her leadership abilities. She also skips the tie-back— that neat summary that brings the answer back to the question asked.*

*A. I'm a strong leader, known for my ability to work effectively with all levels and for my open-door policy. Let me give you an example. When I first started as a manager in the cosmetics industry, I realized that I was going to be dependent on my team—

especially because I was new to the industry. I set up weekly staff meetings, and made sure to listen carefully to the problems my team was encountering. At the same time, I did everything I could to be up-to-date, including reading journals and blogs and attending industry associations. I asked questions and made sure that, from the janitor on up to the executive suite, my door was always open. I'm proud of my ability to establish a climate of trust. *This answer almost makes it, but doesn't really prove her leadership abilities or sell the value of these strengths.*

!A. I'm a strong leader, known for my ability to work effectively with all levels and for my open-door policy. Let me give you an example: When I was fairly new to the cosmetics industry, we had an issue with the quality of one of our products—a skin cream. As the leader of QA (quality assurance) I wanted to set the bar high and make sure that everyone, from our hourly workers, to our top executives, was on board with producing only the very best products. I knew that this was critical to growing our sales and maintaining our reputation. I met with the production team to see if there was any way to salvage the batch, and when it became clear that there were too many problems to ensure the best product, I made the tough decision to toss it. I could have stopped there, but because I'm always thinking of the bottom line, I instituted new quality measures that would prevent this type of problem in the future. This is one example that proves I have the leadership skills to make the critical decisions that ensure quality and strong sales. *This excellent answer uses the power of a specific example to give the interviewer exactly what they need: to see Gladys in action and to deliver proof of her leadership abilities. Remember, generalities don't sell you—specifics do—and when you think of it, Gladys has now given this interviewer an effective way to persuade others that she is the right candidate for the job.*

Ditch It

1. *Why are you asking me about work I did 10 years ago? I can't remember what I did.* Although many of us may have these thoughts, don't admit to them. And never ask an interviewer why they are asking you something unless you need clarification in order to answer the question well. And a second "never": try not to say you can't remember things. However, you could start your answer with something like, "That was a number of years ago, and as I remember the situation, I...." This gives you permission to leave out some of the details.

2. *I don't know what makes me a strong leader. I got promoted and had to figure it out, that's all.* It's wonderful that you got promoted, but you have to be able to talk about yourself and walk the interviewer through an analysis of what makes you tick. It's your job in interviews to provide specific answers with a selling point. You're never not selling!

3. *I make difficult decisions every day. I can't single out a particular example.* Yes you can. This is why your preparation is so critical to interviewing well—you must have a full catalog of resources to use as you answer questions. And if you're asked a question where you really don't have any experience, then say something like: "As I think about it, I've never experienced that exact situation, but I can tell you about something similar." And then tell that story.

Tips

✓ Behavioral interviews are often challenging and exhausting. This is where you must be prepared. I can't tell you how many clients I've had who have debriefed with me after this type of interview and have told me that they did poorly, as they couldn't offer specifics.

✓ Listen carefully and don't start thinking about your answer while the interviewer is still asking the question. Behavioral questions often have more than one part, so hang in there, get the whole question in your mind, and then figure out your best way to answer it.

✓ Keep track of where you are in your answer, but if you get lost and forgot the second or third part of the question, ask the interviewer to please repeat it. You've got plenty of pressure on you already, and it is fine to ask for help.

✓ Use the ZAP technique up front if you are unsure of the question, and use it after your answer if you're worried about whether or not you answered the question well.

✓ Review your list of accomplishment stories that are organized by behavioral topics such as problem-solving, disagreement with a boss, couldn't meet a deadline, and so on, on a daily basis so that these examples are at your fingertips.

15

THE PANEL: ONE OF ME, SO MANY OF YOU

Panel interviews can be a bit scary because it can feel like an inquisition. You have to focus on a number of people at once, and can be uncertain where to look or what to do when panel members give conflicting information.

Let's look at why companies choose this type of interview and how you can best prepare for them. A panel interview does two major things: saves time (everyone is in the room together, which is efficient) and panel interviews allow the group to all have the same experience and to learn from each other's questions as well as the candidate's answers. Let's say the lead interviewer has an aggressive style and shoots out questions in rapid fire. The others on the panel can observe how you respond, as well as how you answer the questions they ask. Some companies find this an easier way to gain a consensus—often right after you leave the room.

Tips for preparing for panel interviews:

✓ As always, research the company and the particular department.

✓ Find out what you can about the panel members (using Google, LinkedIn, and your network).

✓ Think of this experience more like a presentation than an interview, and practice good, solid delivery skills as well as the content (accomplishment stories) for your probable answers (for tips on presentation skills, see Chapters 5 and 21).

✓ If possible, prepare a bit of show and tell. It's amazing how helpful it is to both you and the panel if you can hold up something you've created in the past, whether it's a flow chart or a valve you helped design.

✓ Use your MAP to stay on track and to help reduce nervousness and ask if it's okay to take notes (this gives you a bit of breathing time and helps you remember who said what).

✓ Remember: They wouldn't have invited you in if you weren't a strong candidate, so help them see how you can contribute to the department and company.

✓ Probe for needs politely. You might use a phrase like, "If I understand you correctly, you need a manager who can do x, y, and z. Is that right?"

✓ Use your eye contact strategically. This means look at every member of the panel—always when they're talking—and one thought at a time when you're answering. You may want to give more visual attention to the senior people in the room, but don't let this cause you to ignore anyone. If you do, they won't be voting to have you hired!

Janice's Panel Interview

Let's put this into action. Janice is a Customer Service Representative with 10 years' experience in the telecommunications industry. She is being interviewed by five people (A, B, C, D, and E) from Synergy Inc. and A is the hiring manager. The receptionist brings her into the conference room where the five people are waiting.

A. "Welcome, Janice. Glad you could join us."

Janice: "Very nice to be here." (She makes sure to smile and to look at all five people in the room.)

A. "Please have a seat." (He points to a chair on one side of an oblong table. The five people are spread out opposite her and Janice reminds herself that she will have to turn her head to see the two people to her far left and right.) "We like to have HR start the interview and then we'll all be asking you questions."

B. (The HR person) "Before we get going, could you tell me what happened at Telcordia? I noticed you worked there for ten years. Is that right?"

Janice: "Yes, that is correct. I had a wonderful experience at Telcordia, growing from a Customer Service Representative working mostly on the phones to a manager responsible for a staff of 20. Unfortunately, loss of sales forced the company to make some tough decisions, and streamlining the Customer Service area was one area affected. I'm excited to be looking for a new position where I can use my experience to help another company retain and grow its client base."

B. "Thanks. If I spoke to your most recent boss, what would he or she say about you and why weren't you kept on? I can't believe that a big company like Telcordia could eliminate its entire customer service area."

Janice: (She feels her blood pressure rising and her cheeks burning. This HR person is tough. So she directs her attention to another panel member as she begins her answer and she avoids the clearly evasive "Good question" response that she knows could back fire.) "My most recent boss was Bill Gibbons. We had a wonderful working relationship and I'm confident that he would tell all of you that I'm a highly motivated and effective customer service manager. On one of my performance appraisals he wrote: "Janice is the kind of person this company needs. I wish there were more of her." Regarding the second part of your question (and here Janice looks back at B), I was not privy to the decision that determined who was let go and who stayed or how they will function effectively with reduced staff. But I can tell you without any hesitation (and Janice looks away from B to keep this from becoming a boxing match) that the quality of my work was always excellent. And in fact, Bill is one of my references."

B. "Thanks, Janice. Can you tell me a bit about why you're interested in our company?"

Janice: "I'd be happy to. From what I can tell, Synergy Inc. is poised for a huge increase in sales. You've got a solid foundation and are beginning to take customers from some of the big telecom firms like Telcordia. But this is a juncture where you must also be careful not to lose the benefits of a small, tightly knit group. As an experienced Customer Service Manager I know how to preserve the feeling of "small" while growing big. This is a challenge in which I believe my past experience would be invaluable."

B. "Great answer. Let me turn you over to C."

C. "I still don't get why you were let go? Didn't this have something to do with your performance?" (This is clearly the combative interviewer.)

Janice: "Before I answer you, could you please tell me your name and function? That will help me make sure I address the issues that are important to you." (This is a very smart move, because it creates a buffer between the hostile question and her answer.)

C. "Oh, okay. I'm Jim Black and I'm head of finance."

Janice: "Thank you, Jim. That's helpful. I feel very lucky to have had 10 good years at Telcordia. They hired me right out of college and gave me a solid foundation in the basics of customer service. In addition, they sent me to outside training sessions and promoted me regularly. As we all know, companies have to make tough decisions—especially in this economy. My department was reduced by 50 percent, so I know there is nothing personal about it. It was a business decision, and if I had been upper management, I probably would have done the same thing." (This is a clever answer for a number of reasons: Janice starts with good news and shows sincere appreciation for her former employer. She explains how they invested in her—again proof that she was a valuable employee. Then she adds new information—that half of her department was let go—and demonstrates that she understands the business reasons for the layoffs.)

C. "Well, okay. So what makes you think you can do this job without a lot of supervision?"

Janice: "If I understand Synergy's needs correctly, you're growing so quickly that some aspects of your organization could be compromised. I see Customer Service as the bedrock of a company, because without treating your existing and new customers well, you will lose out to the competition. Let me give you an example from Telcordia that shows not only how I took initiative, but also demonstrates my ability to work effectively with minimum supervision." (Here, Janice uses one of her accomplishment stories to prove this point, and then she consciously ends her answer looking at the boss rather than back at C., who is contentious.)

A." Let's move on to Mary (D.), who would report to the person in this position."

D. "Nice to meet you, Janice. Could you tell me a bit about your management style and how you deal with employees who don't meet your expectations?"

Janice: "Certainly. My management style is open-door and hands-on, while still respecting the integrity of my team. When I first became a manager, I learned how important it is to really know your team, so I scheduled individual sessions with my group in addition to our weekly staff meetings. I was careful to listen and find out the issues that each person wanted to talk about, and to ask for suggestions. I also communicated my style—that I will always assume you can do the job without my help, but that if you need it, never hesitate to ask me. Regarding under performance, I again ask questions first and then create a plan to help the individual meet his or her goals. I have the individual sign the plan so that there is no confusion or mis-understandings. If after this step the problem persists, I again try to find out why and then may have to put that person on probation and have them meet with HR for additional help. I'm happy to say that in my experience it's very rare that problems reach this stage."

C. "That sounds like bullying to me." (The combative interviewer can't resist jumping back in even though it's not his turn.)

Janice looks to A. to see if she should answer this question or let D. continue with her questions.

A. "Let's stick with D's questions for now."

D. "I don't have any other questions. Thanks for your answer, Janice."

Janice: "You are very welcome."

A. "We have one last person, our head of Operations, Sue."

E. "You've answered our questions very thoroughly, so I don't have much to add. But can you tell me how you relate to senior management? What I'm getting at is how you communicate with those people you don't report to, but who are in senior positions."

Janice: "In my experience, that's a critical issue, because Customer Service relates to every aspect of a business. If I ignore sales, for example, I'm not as aware as I need to be with how we're gaining new customers. Or with operations, I of course need to have a clear understanding of how the company is run, as that will have a huge influence on Customer Service. Let me give you an example of a plan that I created that I first submitted to senior management. (And here Janice gives a specific example that proves she is not off on her own ignoring top management.) Did that answer your question?" (It's safe for Janice to ask this of Sue, while it would have been a poor idea with Jim.)

E. "Yes it did. Thank you."

At this point A. gives a short wrap-up and asks Janice if she has any questions. After a few specific ones about the job itself, she asks:

"Would you mind telling me your time frame for making a decision? I'm very excited about this opportunity and know I can ensure that customer service supports your key values as a company." (This is Janice's wrap-up statement.)

A. "We hope to know in about two weeks. We have a few other interviews to conduct and then will meet as a team to make a decision."

Janice: "Thank you very much. Would someone be able to give me everyone's email address so that I can thank each panel member?"

A. "Sure, Janice. I'll make sure that B. (HR) gets those to you. Thanks again for coming in."

Janice stands and then walks over to the other side of the table and shakes each person's hand before leaving. This is another way for her to demonstrate confidence and her strong interest in the firm.

Ditch It!

1. *It doesn't sound to me as if you have a plan for this interview. Why are panel members contradicting each other?* This lack of organization is quite common, but it's not your job to comment on it. You must "sell" yourself effectively despite challenging circumstances.

2. *Is this interview an indication of what it's like to work here? I've never experienced anything like this!* This may be exactly what's going through your mind, but you don't want to share these thoughts at an interview.

3. *I don't have skills in that area.* Of course you aren't going to lie and tell a panel that you can do things that you can't, but when faced with a missing skill, be strategic. You might ask a question, such as "Could you help me understand how that skill is important?" or you could explain that you don't know how to do that but are confident you can learn quickly—and then give an example of how you acquired a new skill at work or school.

Tips

✓   You have some extra preparation to do for panel interviews. These are more like giving a presentation than one-on-one interviews, so your delivery skills must be strong and support your message about your ability to do the job.

✓   Prepare for different styles of interviewers on the panel. Some may be quiet and ask very little, others may take over, and some may want to talk more than ask questions. Keep your cool if challenged by an interviewer, because the group will recognize unfair

behavior and in most cases won't take their criticisms
seriously.

✓ Sit up straight, smile when appropriate, and burn
off your nervous energy by using good volume and
inflection in your voice and by gesturing—making
your key points come alive. (A quick note on smiling:
Some women smile too much when they're nervous,
so watch that you only smile when it makes sense.)

✓ Pay attention to the group dynamics—who is in
charge, how the people on the panel relate to each
other, if they're working as a team or at odds with
each other. It won't be the only information you will
use to make a decision about this company, so these
are important clues that will help you know if this is
a good fit for you.

✓ Watch that your preparation doesn't get in the way
of listening. We work so hard to get ready for interviews, making our MAPS, practicing our accomplishment statements, and researching the company
and the people, that it's easy for our own agenda to
get in the way of paying attention during the interview. Always put good, active listening first.

16

BULL'S-EYE: MEETING WITH THE HIRING MANAGER

There are many paths to the hiring manager: You might get in front of him or her through networking, an online posting or ad, a recruiter, or by targeting a company directly. And some job seekers have met hiring managers at conferences, conventions, or at a ball game. No matter how you got there, this is a critical point in getting an offer, because you're finally in front of the decision-maker.

Before we look at your role as the person being interviewed, let's review some excellent feedback from one of my senior HR clients when I asked her how hiring managers learn how to conduct interviews:

✓ If hiring managers work for a company that uses standard interview guidelines, the hiring manager may or may not use them. When they do use the questions, they often take very few notes, if at all, and fail to ask probing questions to get a complete behavioral example.

✓ Some managers ask a series of hypothetical questions for personal reasons. For example, a young college graduate was asked what she would do as an intern if everyone left the department and she was the only person at work. This interviewer may have experienced a situation in the past where an intern didn't perform up to expectations.

✓ The one thing that interviewers say when they haven't reviewed your resume for more than 30 seconds is "Tell me about yourself" and/or "Walk me through your resume starting with your first job." This gives the interviewer time to quickly review the resume and think of some job-related questions.

✓ Hiring managers interview infrequently. They tend to rely more on "gut" and "fit" than knowledge and skills. Many don't train their leaders how to interview or ask them to take notes. When I have been asked to interview candidates (as the HR Director), no one asked me for behavioral feedback. They simply said, is it yes or no? And we only discussed candidates who the hiring manager was very interested in hiring.

✓ When hiring managers participate in behavioral-focused interview sessions, they quickly forget what they learned if the company culture doesn't reinforce the importance of following the guidelines in the hiring process.

✓ Interviewing is primarily viewed as something that everyone can do that doesn't require any training. Managers develop their own favorite questions and probe in areas that are most important to them. It's probably unusual to see a company that uniformly adheres to a standard approach. For example, in hiring for the sales department at one company where I worked, they were great at training and reinforcing the importance of candidate selection. But the hiring managers in marketing and finance were less concerned and pretty much did their own thing.

This list reinforces one of the key points of this book: Be ready for anything! Also, keep in mind that because of their position, many hiring managers may be pressed for time, letting others in the company explain the details of the job, the company culture, and other issues. What can you do to be ready for this make-or-break interview? My flip answer is: "Everything we've already discussed." My better answer is, if you look back to Part II and review the types of questions, be prepared to go through all these with a hiring manager in less than an hour. But the substance questions (Chapter 8) are where you should put your main focus, because that is where you are proving you can do the job and do it well.

Here's a list of top considerations to concentrate on when interviewing with hiring managers:

- ✓ Watch the structure and length of your answers. Follow a logical sequence like PAR (problem, action, result), and if you're not sure if you gave enough information, ask.
- ✓ Do not try to trick hiring managers. This is a time to be honest about who you are while you "sell" your abilities to them.
- ✓ Never speak negatively about either their company or your former employers. You can admit that there were "challenges," but don't bad mouth anyone.
- ✓ Make sure that your answers demonstrate your critical thinking and problem-solving abilities. This is not the time for off-the-cuff answers or simplistic solutions to complicated problems.
- ✓ Always offer proof where you can. Use the "for example" segue to tell your success stories.
- ✓ Don't act as if you can do everything. You can't, I can't, no one can.

✓ Watch that you don't overuse "we" in your answers. It's great to give credit to your team, but this is your interview, not theirs. Be generous about what others have done, but keep the focus on your individual accomplishments.

✓ Demonstrate that you understand what is needed in the position. If you're unclear, ask the hiring manager for help.

✓ Have thoughtful questions prepared—these will make you look good and may steer the interview in some interesting directions.

✓ In addition to grooming (Chapter 5), make sure you don't smell of cigarettes or strong after shave or perfume. The hiring manager could have allergies or may feel annoyed by these.

✓ In everything you do, from the initial handshake to the last thank you, convey enthusiasm. It's fine to do this in your own style, but it's not optional because this is a key attribute that hiring managers want.

Let's look at how a job candidate might answer a range of questions (and types of questions) from a hiring manager. We'll make the job seeker Barbara, an HR generalist who is meeting with Jane, the head of HR—the person who would be her boss.

Thanks for coming in, today, Barbara. It was nice of Rod to recommend you to us.

Yes, it was. He's been a wonderful help to me in my search.

So before we get going, Barbara, can you tell me why you're no longer with Comcast?

I spent the last four years with Comcast and was promoted twice—most recently into an employee relations and recruitment role. When the HR department was centralized into our headquarters, several positions were cut, including mine. Now I'm looking forward to finding a new position where I can help sustain the strategic management of human resources initiatives.

If I spoke to your most recent boss, what would he or she say about why you were let go?

Did my boss have a role in what happened at Comcast? (Notice this is a rephrase and Barbara does not repeat the negative phrase, "let go.") She was as surprised as I was and apologized over and over for not being able to prepare me. As to what she would say, I know she'd speak very highly of the ways I established trust and positive relations with both management and staff, contributing toward a supportive and productive work environment. Also, she is one of my references, so I'd be very happy if you'd like to have a conversation with her.

I might just do that. So, what do you know about us?

I know you're a Fortune 500 company, and a leader in the publishing industry with a wonderful reputation, especially in books for children. You have innovative programs in the schools to get students excited about reading, and you help schools with limited budgets get the books they so badly need. In terms of your corporate culture, Rod told me that this is a great place to work where employees of all levels are valued. I'm very excited about that.

That was nice of him. Since training and development are part of this position, can you give me some specifics from your background that would prove you're a good fit?

A. Be glad to. I've been involved with training and development my whole career. At Comcast I conducted employee orientations and also ran development and training classes. Some were tailored, so they just had a few people, while other classes were large, with 50 or more participants. My trademark as a trainer is interaction—I'm a strong believer that learning should be hands-on—so I never lecture. I ask questions, encourage ideas from the class, and make sure it's a positive learning experience. This has led to excellent evaluations—helping me know that my training is meeting the participants' needs. Is this in line with what you're looking for?

Yes, yes it is. Let me ask you something a bit different. If you were running this company, what changes would you make?

I don't know enough about your Human Resources Department to answer that, but I can tell you about some of the changes I've initiated in the past—and these would be a good predictor of my future performance. At Comcast I initiated a mentoring program for new hires, as our retention rate was low. I paired new people up with employees who had been with the company for a while, and created a schedule of events or meetings to ensure that the new hires had all the support they needed. In the first year, this was so successful, our retention rate increased by more than 60 percent, and an interesting side effect of this program was a huge improvement in morale. From our employee surveys we learned that we had become a better place to work. I also suggested a policy to include HR in more of the company's strategic decisions. I can't tell you how that worked out because I left only two months after it was implemented. I hope these examples give you a sense of changes I might make if your needs are similar.

Thanks, Barbara. Good answer. What's the last book you read and what did you like about it?

A. I just read an amazing book titled *Following Atticus* which I stumbled upon by chance. It's about a reporter and his dog, and it turns into an adventure story as they hike the White Mountains in New Hampshire. It's as much a personal journey as it is a wilderness saga and I loved the way the two parts of the book were intertwined. Both the reporter and his dog were unlikely heroes and went way beyond what they thought they could do.

It looks as if you've been out of work for more than a year. Is there something wrong with you and why should I hire you?

A. I'm happy to tell you why my search has taken awhile and what makes me a great fit for your company. When I was let go I took some time to think carefully about what I wanted in my next position. Although my most recent work has been in employee relations and recruitment, I'm seeking a broader generalist role. I like to be challenged in different ways and enjoy the stimulation of wearing many hats. Because I'm not looking to step into a role exactly like my last one, my search has taken a bit longer. To answer the second part of your question, why you should hire me, it's simple—I can do this job and do it well. And I bring a background that makes getting up-to-speed easy. From everything I've learned so far, this is a wonderful fit and I know I could help your HR department meet its goals.

Last question, Barbara. What would someone who doesn't like you say about your performance?

A. How would a coworker who sees things differently than I do, describe me? (Note: Here is the rephrase helping Barbara out of a tight spot.) The feedback that I've received through the course of my career is that I'm highly motivated and also fair. I understand this doesn't always make me popular with everyone, but it does mean I'm respected. I've learned a great deal from people who don't agree with me and I value diverse opinions. At the end of the day, I think we're all better for being exposed to each other's ideas, and my track record of innovation within Human Resources proves that my interpersonal skills help me work effectively with all personalities and levels.

Thanks so much for coming in today. We'll be back in touch in a few weeks.

Is it all right if I follow up with you in about 10 days? I'm very excited about this position and I'd love to work here.

Yes, that's fine. We'll be in touch.

Thanks very much, Jane. I look forward to the next steps. (Barbara shakes her hand and leaves her office.)

What I hope you notice while reading through this script is how quickly a hiring manager may move from one type of question to another, and how Barbara, the candidate, uses many of the techniques we've discussed. When she needs more information she asks a question back or ZAPs, when challenged she uses a rephrase, and at every point where she can, she "sells" her background with specific examples and demonstrates enthusiasm for the job.

What makes this more challenging is that I can't tell you what will happen to you in your interviews with hiring managers. That is why excellent preparation, understanding the types of questions you may be asked, and having a broad range of interview skills will help you be ready for anything. And it's also why memorizing answers to the questions you think you might be asked is a poor idea. The chances of your knowing what you'll be asked are very slim. But let's say you have an inside contact who gets you the questions ahead of time (and this has happened to a few of my clients). You still have to demonstrate that you can think on your feet. You want to come across as a person who is present and actively listening. Use whatever information you have before an interview to be as ready as possible, but be careful to come into the interview without preconceived ideas. It's often a wild ride.

Why Won't You Just Hire Me?

Joan had basically worked for one organization—a top university. She loved her work in public relations and had been promoted to Assistant Director. She had a broad background in communications, event planning, and public affairs, and saw herself as an indispensable part of her department. Then, on a day filled with meetings and more work than she could possibly handle, she was called into the Dean's office and saw that a representative from HR was there as well. She was going to be late for her next meeting and figured that whatever this was would only take a moment.

She was asked to sit down and was then was told that her job was being eliminated as part of a campus-wide reduction in expenses.

"What?" she had asked.

The HR person repeated the message and added that she could finish out the six weeks until the end of the year, and then would have a severance package.

"Who is going to do the work?" she demanded, looking at the Dean. The Dean looked down at his papers.

"We have made arrangements for that. What we'd like you to do now is go to the conference room. We have a career coach there who will talk to you about your outplacement program. When you're done there, please come to my office and we'll review your benefits, including your severance package."

"This isn't right."

The HR person spoke again. "We understand this is a shock and it's very important that you know that this has nothing to do with your performance."

"Is Cindy being let go?" Joan was now boiling inside and wanted to know if the new hire who did very little work was keeping her job.

"I'm sorry, Joan," said the HR person, "but I can't share any of that information with you. Why don't I walk you to the conference room?"

Joan glared at the Dean, who still had his head buried in his papers and left the room.

Fast forward a month and Joan and I have met several times. We've talked about the shock and hurt and the steps she can take now to protect herself as she finishes out her work with the university. We've written a first draft of her resume and have begun to work on her goals or plan for her search. This became a challenge because Joan only wanted to work for the university where she had spent the past 17 years. She didn't believe that any other school would be as good a place to work and she was resentful that she had been let go.

Several weeks later, she had an interview with the Dean of another department. (Because she still had access to inside information, this was for a position that wasn't posted yet.) She created her MAP, we practiced her accomplishment stories, she researched the department and the Dean, and we reviewed her physical skills to ensure that she appeared upbeat and motivated.

The results were frustrating. The Dean for this new opportunity couldn't be pinned down. She complimented Joan on her contributions to the university, and even went so far as to say that Joan would be a good fit for her department, but was evasive regarding her time table for filling the position. Joan sent a well-thought-out thank-you email the next day, put a note on her calendar to follow up the next week, and obsessed about the position. Her last six weeks on the job were awful. She felt shunned by the others in her department and she refused to talk with her Dean. She somehow got her work done, but couldn't move past her resentment.

As she and I continued to meet to review her search, I suggested she contact some other universities and look for ways to expand her possible opportunities. She refused. She had to have this one job and have it now. There was a brief period of false hope as the Dean for the new position checked Joan's references, but then she was met with deafening silence. She tried following up by email, but there was no response. She called—again no response. Boiling over with frustration, she walked over to the Dean's office and was told by her administrative assistant that she was busy.

"Why won't they hire me?" she asked me. "They know the work I've done and what I can do and they're not going to find anyone better. I just don't get it."

"I can't answer that," I told her, "as I don't have inside information. You and I both know that in general, academia moves pretty slowly, so they could be interested in you, but it might take months. Or they might already have someone else in mind. To protect yourself, my advice is move on, get your focus on some new opportunities, so that you're not stuck waiting to hear from this Dean."

"But I don't want to!"

"I don't blame you one bit, but the only way to get past what has happened to you—to get beyond the hurt and anger and resentment—is to fill the pipeline, look for other opportunities, and expand your network. You might be surprised at what will happen."

Joan looked at me and shook her head. I could see that she thought I was nuts. But once she had completed her six weeks, once she was home and no longer at the university, she began to get it. She added private schools to her target list and before long discovered that a school less than two miles from her home was looking for a public relations manager. She answered the ad, received a call less than a week later, and had an interview. As I helped her prepare for the interview, I reminded her not to compare this school to her university because I knew that would pull her back into feeling resentful and angry. Joan agreed and did a fantastic job at the two rounds of interviews. What stood out for her was that the hiring manager wanted her—he confirmed her value and her accomplishments—and was excited about having someone like her at the school.

When we reviewed the offer, she shook her head at the salary—it was considerably less than what she had been making. So I asked her what would off-set that. What were the other benefits of this job? Aside from the easy commute, it would give her the chance to be a big fish in a small pond and it would also give her the opportunity to wear many hats—something that happens often with smaller organizations. The real plus, as she saw it, was working in a more collaborative and supportive culture with a boss who valued her contributions. Although she had loved her work at the university, she understood now that the politics and competitiveness had made her job difficult.

Ditch It!

1. *Why would you look at another candidate when you know I can do the job?* The issue here is tone—this is a combative question—and it's really none of your business to refer to other candidates.

2. *How did you get promoted to this position?* Again, none of your business. A safer question would be: "How long have you been with the company?" and if you wanted to be super-safe, you could add "Do you mind my asking how long you've been with the company?"

3. *My last boss thought I was a great fit and all my references can testify that I can do this job. Why don't you?* What your last boss or your references think aren't relevant at the moment. You must convince the hiring manager—that person who would be your boss—that you're the best candidate for the job. And don't forget, he or she must "like" you and must feel that you will be a good person to work with. Avoid questions that back this critical person into a corner; it won't make them want to hire you.

Tips

✓ Meeting with the hiring manager is the heart of the interview. Do everything you can to make this individual see that you can do the job, do it well, and love to do it. (This is also true when you meet with a person above the hiring manager.)

✓ Be prepared for surprises. Interviewing is such an unpredictable process, watch that you don't have preconceptions about your interviews with hiring managers, because that can make it harder to adjust to the actual interview.

✓ Balance confidence with willingness to learn. In other words, you might find it helpful to tell yourself before this critical interview, "They'd be lucky to have me," but don't let that confidence-builder turn into arrogance. You could be very lucky to work with them, and it won't hurt if you demonstrate that you feel this way. Appreciation is gold.

✓ Do your best to stay neutral during the actual interview. This does not mean you should take abuse, which is a rare occurrence, but don't react negatively to questions that may be designed to test your professionalism.

✓ Listen, listen, and listen. Quality listening is one of the best skills you can demonstrate during an interview and it will help you uncover the real needs of the job and make you come across as a motivated and concerned candidate.

✓ If asked something you can't answer, do your best to address the question without using a flat-out "No, I never did that." As you know from your preparation (Part I), you can ZAP or ask a question, rephrase the question to turn it to your advantage, or find a way to build a bridge from what you know to what you don't know. And your ace in the hole is your ability to learn new things quickly. Make sure you have an example of this handy.

✓ Burn off your nervousness by paying attention and using good physical skills: posture, gesture, voice, and eye contact. You should be nervous—this is a high stakes game—but you don't want it to get in the way. And use your MAP for reassurance. If your mind goes blank or you wonder if you just gave a certain example, glance down at your MAP. By checking off the examples or accomplishments as you give them, you don't have to worry about repeating yourself. (This typically becomes an issue in all-day interviews where you might be meeting with the hiring manager at the end of the day when you're exhausted. See if you can get five minutes before this critical meeting to eat your power bar, drink some water, look at your MAP, and you'll be good to go.)

17

PRESENTATIONS

A nerve-racking part of an interview, presentations put job candidates at center stage where they must demonstrate that they not only know their subject matter, but that they also know how to deliver that information in an interesting and logical way. This is one of the few times in the interview process when the candidate is in charge. Most commonly part of scientific interviews, presentations may be required in other areas such as training, teaching, or sales.

What are the keys things to consider when giving an interview presentation?

- ✓ Pick a topic that you know inside-out and that is as relevant to the job as possible.
- ✓ Make sure you know how long you should speak.
- ✓ Settle the question of handouts ahead of time (who will make copies and when the audience will receive them). In scientific presentations it is customary to email your presentation to the company a week before

your interview so that those who will be attending can look at it beforehand and can take notes on a copy during the presentation. Be careful that the handouts don't eclipse your speech. When possible, give them out at the end or offer to post them on your website or the company's website.

✓ Get to the interview early so that you can take care of any logistics (setting up the equipment, arranging the chairs in the conference room, and so on).

✓ Have a back-up plan in case technology fails. This is where having copies could give you an alternate way to present.

✓ Decide when you want questions (I love them during a presentation but some prefer them after. It's your show, set the rules up front.)

✓ Have a plan to reduce nervousness at the beginning. Will someone introduce you? One client of mine asked each person for a 15-second introduction before he started his presentation. This created a collaborative tone and helped him feel a bit less tense. This obviously isn't practical with a large audience.

What is your ending strategy and how are you going to get your audience to start asking questions? (One great trick is to have a question or two that you can ask them, such as, "How many of you were surprised by the results of the initial study?" By holding up your hand when you ask this question, you'll get at least a few people to raise their hands and that breaks the ice.)

As a scientific candidate you might be in a large conference room or an auditorium presenting to 50 or more people. And these aren't just any people—they're scientists and they're people who will know if your research is flawed. Most companies, recognizing this pressure, schedule the presentation for late morning—after you've met with the hiring manager and one or two others—often HR—but before lunch and before you get tired.

Sometimes a person who is part of the interview team takes a challenging or combative approach to see how you, the candidate, react to stress. But much more often the interviewers and others in the audience understand how tough this situation is for you and are kind. A neighbor of mine who is a biologist working for a major pharmaceutical firm told me that she recently asked a candidate to explain a few things that were unclear in his presentation. But she did this privately and told him that she understood how tough giving the presentation was.

Just Exactly How Good Are You, Anyway?

Here's an example of giving a presentation as part of an interview that I experienced in the past year. A military sub-contractor placed an ad in the local paper where I had recently relocated, for a trainer with a career counseling background. I read through the job requirements carefully and saw that I matched all of them except one—military experience. I also had quite a bit more counseling experience than was listed, but figured it would be good to give it a try because I was new to the area. I tailored my resume and wrote a careful cover email expressing my interest in the position and how my background fit their needs.

Two weeks later I received a call from the hiring manager at the sub-contracting firm asking for a date for an initial phone screening. We set the time and date and I prepared by researching the company as well as what the clients (military personnel) might need. I had all my information in front of me including my interview MAP and resume, had my headset on, and waited for my phone to ring. The interviewer (let's say her name is Cathy), called 10 minutes late and started her list of questions with no ice breaker, no small talk. Her first question was about compensation, and I was careful to ask her what her range was. It was low, and when I asked, Cathy told me that there was no room for negotiation. I said that I was confident we could work out a fair agreement and she moved on to her next questions. It was clear to me that she was reading off a list and that she didn't want much background—just yes or no answers. Some of her questions felt like trick ones, like "Name the three kinds of resumes," but I didn't have any problems answering them. Cathy told me that I would have time at the end to ask her questions, but she cut the call short after setting up a date for a second phone screening.

The second screening was very much like the first: dry, impersonal, and what I would call a shot-gun approach as Cathy asked questions one right after the other and clearly was rushed and didn't want to engage in conversation. I adapted my style to hers, made an effort to stay upbeat, and toward the end of the call, she told me that they would like to bring me in for an in-person interview. She gave me a website that would provide background information on their programs, and told me that I would need to give a 10-minute presentation as part of the interview. She would email me the topics I could choose from, and I would have to submit my presentation at least a week before the interview.

I picked the topic that I liked best—what makes an effective job search—and worked on my PowerPoint presentation. I used military terminology where appropriate and tailored my visuals to what I knew about this audience. My first visual had my photo and the name of the sub-contractor plus the date and the title of my presentation. It was quite an interesting experience to walk into the conference room on the day of my interview and see my photo on the screen.

Here's where the logistics became complicated. Cathy was on speaker phone (she was several hundred miles away) as was a secondary hiring manager from the sub-sub contractor. In the room were three women—one was a trainer with the same organization from another state, and the other two were part of the career services at the military base. Cathy asked me to introduce myself to the women in the room, and then give my presentation. I asked if they would like me to keep track of the time, or if someone else would. The trainer in the room volunteered, so I was good to go. I made sure that the spider phone was close to the front of the room and discovered, about halfway through my presentation, that Cathy and her counter-part also had my PowerPoint in front of them.

I kept my explanations brief, and focused on how to help military personnel adjust to being in transition. At the end, I thanked them for the opportunity to present and asked if anyone had any questions. Cathy said that there was no time for questions, but that she'd like me to rate my own presentation using a 1 to 10 scale. After I had given myself a 9 out of 10 and explained why, she said that the interview was over and that I would hear back from them, either way, by the end of the week. As I gathered up my materials, I showed the women in the room a copy of my book (as nothing beats show and tell). They were quite interested in it and started asking questions, but Cathy quickly reminded them that they had other candidates waiting and to wrap things up.

I sat in my car and did my post-interview debrief, starting with what I had done well. I had given a strong and on-target presentation, I wasn't thrown by the two decision-makers not being in the room, I stayed within my 10-minute timeframe, and demonstrated both experience and passion for helping those in transition. On the "what I might do differently next time" list I put: include my book as part of the PowerPoint, create better questions for them (although there probably wasn't time for this), and go in with lower expectations. In my excitement at having an interview, I had glossed over the fact that this job wasn't a good fit. (Pay was one part of that, but going back to a training role felt limiting when I was used to more diversity and responsibility.) I put my notes away and ate a nice big piece of dark chocolate that I had bought earlier just for this moment, and drove home thinking how odd it was that I had been asked to grade my own presentation. And just so you know the end of the story, I didn't get an offer but gained interview practice and learned a few things. Not bad.

Let's look at a few questions that a presenter might receive during or after a presentation.

Thanks, Barry, for explaining that clinical trial to us. If you did such a good job at your last company, why did they let you go?

+A. Well, that's hard to answer as I wasn't part of the decision-making process. But it sure didn't have anything to do with my work. *A weak answer, Barry doesn't give any information that would persuade the group that his work is excellent.*

*A. Did my performance have anything to do with what happened at XYZ? Absolutely not. Small drug companies have to make tough decisions, and cutting my job and several other senior scientist roles was just part of a business decision to keep the company afloat. *Right to the point, this is a bit better but runs the risk of sounding a bit blunt.*

!A. Why was I released after leading a successful clinical trial? (Here is a rephrase helping Barry turn this negative question around.) First, let me say that I what I learned at XYZ was invaluable. I was asked to lead this trial because of my background with statins, and helped launch one of the company's most successful drugs. But as you all know, this is a tough market for new drugs with so many blockbusters coming off patent. When the company had to make cuts, many senior positions were affected, including mine. This is just the way business is done and I didn't take it personally. Now I'm looking forward to being part of a drug discovery team where I can continue to make a difference. *Maybe a bit long, Barry demonstrates strong confidence in his skills and abilities as he explains what happened to his last job.*

Why didn't you give credit to the other researchers on your team?

+A. Hey, they're not the ones looking for a job. *While true, this defensive answer would make most interviewers dislike this candidate.*

*A. I didn't mean to leave them out, it's just that I was talking about the work I did, and to keep within your time limit, I couldn't explain what role others had in my work. *Never use time or the interviewer's parameters for the interview as an excuse. As a professional you should know how to be successful in many different situations.*

!A. What role did my team members play in my research? When you look at scientific work, most of us quickly realize that our individual contributions are part of something bigger. We're dependent on those who have come before, as well as on our teams and colleagues. In terms of credit, in my published papers and abstracts, you'll see a careful system of notation so that each person gets credit for what he or she contributed. A presentation, however, is a more like a conversation, so the footnotes or references may come later or not at all. Is there a specific question I can answer? *Here, using a rephrase and a ZAP, Barry carefully explains how his ideas are linked to others and how he attributes credit. Note how powerfully these two techniques neutralize a negative question.*

Can we have the handouts now?

+A. No, I'd rather give them to you at the end so that you'll pay attention to me. *Although truthful, this answer is going to make the audience dislike the speaker or presenter.*

*A. Gosh, I know it's useful to have them to take notes on, but I'd rather give them to you at the end. *A tiny bit better, this answer is less blunt, but again would create resentment.*

!A. When should handouts be given out? Studies have shown that handouts are often distracting because they pull the audience's attention away from the speaker. I have prepared copies for all of you which I'll give out as soon as my talk is over, and I promise that if there are any issues that are confusing, I'll stay after to make sure they're resolved. Also, if anything is unclear as I go through my presentation, please stop me and I'll make sure to explain it. *Here is a presenter/job candidate in control, illustrating both confidence and concern. Notice how the rephrase doesn't use a pronoun—doesn't turn this into a personal struggle with the questioner—but rather broadens the issue to the ideal time to provide handouts. This would not be an appropriate answer for scientific presentations because the audience expects them before the talk.*

I didn't understand what you said about training new hires. Is that relevant to this position?

+A. Sure it is. With any new program you've got to find a way to get people on board, so training is important and that's an area where I have excellent skills. *The candidate misses an opportunity here to dig deeper and to get this person on his or her side.*

*A. I'm sorry if anything was unclear. Let me try to explain it a bit better. If I understand this project correctly, it's going to require additional resources, such as new hires to help us meet these aggressive goals. The training I was referring to is on-boarding— the process of bringing new people up to speed. *Very polite in tone and taking full responsibility for the "misunderstanding," this answer is much more likely to create an ally because it doesn't insult the questioner. Even if an audience member asks a stupid or insulting question, you can't attack him or her, or the whole audience will turn on you.*

!A. Would training new hires be an important part of this position? I'm sure you know the answer to this much better than I do, and I apologize if it sounded as if I made an assumption. What I was thinking was that with the new project, you would probably have to increase your staff and that would mean getting new people trained quickly. Would this be part of the Project Manager's role? *Using a rephrase and a ZAP, this answer must be given with open and friendly body language so that it doesn't escalate conflict with the questioner. The initial rephrase gives the job candidate think-ing time and the ZAP at the end respectfully asks for clarification.*

Where did you get that information?

+A. Off the internet. Isn't it accurate? *This is a dangerous ZAP because it challenges the questioner.*

*A. I spent a lot of time on your company website and then used Google to find additional sources. I also checked out a few industry blogs to see what I could learn about your company. *A bit better because there's more information, this answer may not address the underlying issue behind this question: Is the information accurate?*

!A. What sources did I use to find this information? First let me say that I hope you'll correct me if any of my information is inaccurate. In preparing for this interview and presentation I read everything I could get my hands on about your company and about the challenges of marketing probiotic products. In addition to what I found online, I spoke to experts in the field, includ-ing Dr. Jones, who confirmed that I was on target with the main points in my presentation. I'm very excited about these products because I'm confident they will have a huge influence in keeping people healthy. *Here we see how a skilled interviewer/presenter takes a potentially hostile question and turns it to his or her advantage while answering the key concept of the question. Think about what the inter-viewers now know about this candidate. He or she is highly motivated, intelligent, and a go-getter who wants this job.*

Ditch It!

1. *Weren't you paying attention to my presentation? I ex-plained that point several times.* You may have to ex-plain a point 10 times, but don't let that throw you. Never challenge your audience in this negative way.

2. *From everything I've read, your methodology is wrong.* You don't have to agree to anything that you think is incorrect, just be diplomatic about the way you do it. Asking a question here would be a better way to go.

3. *It's really rude to be doing something on your Blackberry during my presentation. Could you please turn it off?* Yikes—this is a full fist fight. Improve your presentation skills and keep your visuals short and interesting, and you should be able to get most of your audience to pay attention. If you notice that you're losing a majority of the people, stop and ask them a question and get them engaged.

Tips

✓ Take care of the logistics of presenting ahead of time and get to your interview early so that you can make sure the room and equipment are set up the way you want them.

✓ Find out if someone will introduce you. This makes the transition to presenting a bit smoother.

✓ Ramp your energy up into high gear for presenting. It's a performance, and as I tell my clients, "If you're not going to be interesting, send an email."

✓ Rehearse your talk many times so that you're comfortable with it. As you rehearse, think about your gestures—what are the key points that need to come alive?

✓ Make sure that your visuals don't compete with you. Keep them simple, colorful, and use pictures instead of words when you can. If you have a complicated chart with a ton of data on it, give an overview first, skip the details if you can, and reassure your audience that they will receive a copy of this in their handouts.

- ✓ Increase the volume and inflection of your voice because you're now at the front of the room and must command attention. This often solves the "Blackberry" problem mentioned in Ditch It!
- ✓ Use a raised hand to control when you get questions if you need to. In general, this isn't necessary when there are fewer than 15 people in the room, but if you get one of those non-top talkers, it's a good devise. And of course don't look back at the talker unless you want more questions from him or her.
- ✓ If there are samples you can use so that you're including "show and tell" in your presentation, then do it. It's a powerful way to make ideas or concepts come alive.

18

WHEN THERE'S TRAVEL, MEALS, SKYPE, OR ASSESSMENTS

On top of all the stress of interviewing, you now have some additional logistics to worry about. How are you going to get to the interview? When will you have time to eat? What's safe to order? If the interviewer orders a glass of wine, should you? What if it's a Skype interview—how can you prepare for that? Or what should you do if you suddenly have to take a test?

First of all, don't panic. You aren't the first job candidate to face these challenges and you won't be the last. In general, your common sense will get you successfully through most of these situations. Let's look at travel first. You live in Rhode Island and a company in Nevada wants you to fly out for an interview. (You have probably passed at least one phone screening before this happens.) If there is a recruiter involved, he or she should handle the logistics. But don't be shy if a particular airport is easier for you to get to—just ask politely if you can use the one you want—and ask about how you should get to the airport. Should you hire a car service or take your own car and put it in long-term parking? Keep receipts for anything you pay for yourself, keep track of your mileage, and know before the trip, how, and when you'll be reimbursed.

Try to ensure that your travel arrangements are as stress free as possible. Don't plan to land in Reno at 2 p.m. for a 3 p.m. interview—that's way too risky and you'll be looking at your watch the entire flight wondering if you're going to make it. Wear clothes that are comfortable but that you could wear to the interview if your bag is lost. (If you can carry on your interview clothes, that's a bit safer, but don't forget you might meet someone from the company on the plane or at the airport, so ditch those old jeans with holes in them.) Have phone numbers programmed into your cell phone so that you can easily reach someone if there's a problem. Put any medications you might need in your purse or carry-on bag so that if a health issue flares up on the flight, you can take care of it.

If you have to rent a car to get to the company's office in Reno, get good directions so that you won't be worrying about getting lost. Few rental cars come with a GPS, so either bring your own or use a phone app such as Google Maps. Always have a snack with you in case your plane is late or you don't have time to eat during the flight (check your teeth after you eat). Review your interview MAP and notes on the company during your trip.

Once you arrive at the company parking lot, take a few minutes to breathe, relax, and get ready for the interview. It's amazing how effective a short pause can be. Rushing from the car into the building is not going to help you feel confident. (This is why it's so important to avoid travel logistics that lead to this kind of stress.) Enter the building about 10 to 15 minutes early, but not more as that can create pressure for the interviewer. Greet the receptionist and say who you are and why you're here. Ask for the restroom if you need to freshen up. If you're more comfortable sitting down, that's fine, but don't unpack your portfolio or purse and don't cross your legs. If you prefer to stand (as I do), then stand near a seat where you can rest your portfolio and purse so that your hands are free when the interviewer comes to get you.

Back in Chapter 5 we looked at first impressions—make these powerful first moments work for you by smiling and offering a firm handshake. Look happy to be there even if you're a wreck inside. Establish solid eye contact with the person who has come to get you. And if you're asked about your flight, give a positive answer (see Chapter 6 for ice-breaker questions and ways to answer them). You've now done everything you can do get off to a good start: you arrived on time or a bit early, you've given yourself enough time so that even if the plane is late, you're not, and you've had water and a snack or a meal so that you'll have the energy and stamina for the interview.

But what if, despite your best plans, you can't make it to the interview on time? As soon as you can, call your contact person and explain what has happened. You aren't responsible for the weather or airline delays. (Although you might ask for the interview to be rescheduled if you know there's a strong probability of a blizzard or tornado.) It's now their problem to figure out how you're going to see eight different people in less time. If possible, you can offer to stay an additional day to make this easier. Going back to Chapter 1, your interview MAP is your life raft—this careful preparation will save you when the interviews have to be compressed or when you have an all-day interview. Why? Because the MAP demonstrates fit (the company's needs on one side, your accomplishments on the other) and allows you to keep track of what you've said to whom. This is particularly helpful when you find yourself getting tired and unfocused.

Now you're halfway through your all-day interview, and you're invited to have lunch with the hiring manager and a few others. You follow them to the company cafeteria or you're driven to a near-by restaurant. You should order something you like that isn't messy or the most expensive item on the menu. Spaghetti is a bad idea as it's likely to end up on your suit, but a sandwich, soup, or a simple entree (not ribs) is just fine. If the others order an alcoholic beverage, ask for iced tea, water, or soda, as you can't afford to lose your edge. If this is a dinner meeting after your full day of interviews and the others are drinking wine or beer, you can order one, but watch that you don't drink more than you can safely handle. (For me, that's about three sips. I'm a cheap date.)

Now is the time to remember everything your mother told you about table manners: wait for the others to eat first, keep your elbows off the table, take small bites, and chew with your mouth closed. I was recently at a networking lunch and my friend was done with his meal while I had barely started mine. I got time to eat by saying, "I'd like to hear about your new job. How's it going?" My best advice for interview meals is don't expect to eat much. That's why you eat a good meal before the interview and carry high-energy snacks with you. Lastly, watch your caffeine intake if you're sensitive to it. You don't need something that makes you feel wired up or shaky.

Now let's discuss video interviews that use technology to bring you and the interviewers together. Skype or a webcam offers you and the interviewers the chance to see each other, and to "meet" in real time even though you're thousands of miles apart or in different countries. Some companies start with a one-way process for screening interviews, meaning they can see you but you can't see them, but the more frequently used form of video interviewing is two-way. You may be in a professional setting, such as a recruiter's office or at a company that offers video conferencing, or you may be at home using your own equipment. Here are some tips to get through the interview.

- ✓ Understand how the technology works and practice if possible. Many people have either a webcam or Skype on their home computers, or you could go to a place that offers video conferencing and ask if you can practice.
- ✓ Confirm the time and make sure you and the interviewer understand the difference in time zones. I almost missed my Skype interview for my CMF

certification because my evaluator was in the Netherlands and hadn't put "a.m." or "p.m." after the time. I sent him a confirmation email the day before the interview and we got it straightened out.

✓ Position the camera so that you're visible from the waist up. Make sure that the top of your head isn't cut off and watch that what is behind you—the background—isn't distracting. This is called framing.

✓ Watch the lighting. If there's a window behind you, chances are your face will be in shadow and the background could be distracting.

✓ Check the sound ahead of time if possible. If the microphone is close to you, watch that you don't shuffle your papers and make distracting noises such as coughing or clicking your pen. And make sure to put your cell phone and/or house phone on silent.

✓ Try to get the names of the people who will be interviewing you and add them to your MAP. This will help you relate to them and feel a bit more comfortable.

✓ Moderate your gestures to fit within the screen and make sure they are productive gestures, not nervous flapping.

✓ Never touch your face or your hair. This is distracting.

✓ Establish good solid eye contact with the interviewer or interviewers. Try to forget about the technology and simply talk to this person or people. As in a live interview, it's critical to create rapport and pay attention to what they want. Your eyes help you do this.

✓ Eliminate the possibility of any disturbances. Because it was hot when I had my Skype interview for my certification, I left the door to my office open and my dog came into the room when we were almost done. My interviewer was luckily amused, and wanted me to move my laptop so that he could see the dog. As I did this I remembered that I had only dressed up from the waist up—pearls and a nice blouse—but on my lower half I had on shorts and sandals. I sat down as quickly as I could and never found out if he had seen my casual side.

✓ Tell the interviewers if you're having technical difficulties, such as not being able to see them or a huge lag between your answers and their questions. If these problems can't be resolved, see if you can have the interview rescheduled. It's way too stressful to be at your best when you're fighting technology.

✓ Adapt to the interviewer or interviewers' style. If they are formal, be formal back. If they want short answers, provide them. If they seem chatty and informal, relax a bit, but don't be fooled by friendly behavior—you're still on the hot seat.

Lastly, some coaches recommend using the "picture-in-picture" feature, which allows you to see yourself (it's basically a window at the bottom of the screen). I think this is a bad idea because it's distracting to see yourself while you're interviewing. Your focus should always be on them, not you. (This is why it's difficult to have dinner with someone when there is a mirror behind you. The other person is likely to be admiring his or her hair instead of listening to you.)

Another interview challenge can be assessments. Used frequently with sales professionals, assessments and other tests can be part of the interview process for a wide range of positions. Constructed for reliability and validity, the main reason they're used is to provide information on a potential candidate and to give the hiring company a more objective and better way to hire. Administrative candidates are often tested on Microsoft Office or on scheduling or financial software to ensure they can do what their resume says they can do, while top executives may be required to take a personality or cognitive assessment to give the recruiter and the hiring company in-depth information before getting to the next stage. And sometimes, as with writers, editors, and graphic designers, the test is not a formal assessment, but simply an on-the-spot assignment that proves they can do the work.

Why would companies go to the trouble and expense of having assessments as part of the interview? Very simply because it's more expensive to hire the "wrong" person. In Chapter 5 we looked at the power of first impressions, and what we have to remember here is that the interviewers may decide that they "like" us in the first few seconds and this may cloud their judgment. In other words, the hiring process isn't entirely logical. Feelings may override facts. A good candidate who is soft spoken might be overlooked, while a weak candidate who shows confidence gets hired. Companies spend billions of dollars annually fixing these mistakes.

What you need to remember if assessments are part of your search is that they are just another way for you to explain who you are. And perfection is not what companies are looking for, so take that pressure off yourself and don't try to second-guess the test. In fact, many instruments are set up to flag the test taker who "plays the test." You are who you are and your goal in taking an assessment is to offer the hiring company another way to see that.

The two most common types of instruments used in hiring are ability or cognitive tests that gauge your verbal, mathematical, and abstract reasoning skills, and personality assessments that look into how you relate to others, your outlook on life, the way you solve problems, your preferred work environments, and your feelings. There are too many different types of assessments to cover them carefully here, but a few examples, used most often with executive candidates are the Hogan Personality Inventory, Raven's Progressive Matrices, and the Wonderlic WPT-R Test. Take a look at *Employment Personality Tests Decoded*, by Anne Hart with George Sheldon for more information.

A Travel Nightmare

Traveling to interviews adds a great deal of drama to an already tense situation. Let me tell you about Kate, who had to travel from New Jersey to Dallas, Texas, for an interview as a sales representative. She had done careful research, we had practiced her accomplishment examples, and she had an interview MAP for each person she was scheduled to meet with. We had even talked about what she was going to wear, so I was confident things would go very well.

Kate got to her hotel around 8:30 p.m. the night before her interview, had a light supper from room service, unpacked her clothes, and went over her materials one last time. She set an alarm on her cell phone and used the clock radio in her room to set a second one just to be sure she'd wake up on time. In the morning, she got up early feeling relaxed and rested. She took a shower and then looked for the hair dryer, suddenly discovering that there wasn't one in her bathroom. She called the main desk and they told her that they didn't have hair dryers. Now she was in panic mode. She threw on her travel clothes, rushed out to the parking lot, and drove to a near-by mall to purchase a hair dryer. She found a store that was open early, got an inexpensive hair dryer, and rushed back to her hotel. Now she barely had time to dry her hair, put on her make-up, and get dressed. She checked out of the hotel, rushed back out to her car, and drove to the interview, which was less than a mile away. She felt jittery and distracted.

The problem went from bad to worse as the day progressed, because she hadn't had time to eat breakfast and she had forgotten an important part of interview preparation—having a high-protein snack. The company offered her coffee, but she was afraid to drink it on an empty stomach, so only drank water. By 2 p.m. (and yes companies do forget that you need to eat lunch) she could barely talk and she knew her answers were rambling and disorganized. She was upset with herself, which only made matters worse. When it was finally over, she drove back to the airport, returned her car, and at 4 p.m. had her first meal of the day. She didn't get the job.

In reviewing this experience with her, we agreed there were a few things she could have done to avoid the problems she encountered: get to the hotel earlier in the day, so that if there were things she needed, she would have time to get them then, bring a snack as an emergency food back-up, and call the hotel before the trip to ask what they provided. She and I agreed that this was an unfortunate experience and I'm sure it never happened to her again.

Ditch It!

1. *I can't hear you! Do you have your volume turned up?* Of course it's critical to be able to hear the interviewer, but if there are technical difficulties, explain this in a calm and professional way.

2. *Gosh, this camera makes me look fat. I'm really not that big!* Yes, the camera does add a bit of weight to our images, but don't comment on it. This is not the time to worry about how you look. Get the focus on what the interviewer needs.

3. *Boy, the wings look good. Have you had them?* Chatty and informal in tone, this isn't a good question, because you shouldn't be eating wings at an interview. Stick to foods that you can eat with a fork or a spoon or something that won't get all over you.

4. *How can anyone get anywhere on time with these darned airlines?* Yes, you can be frustrated, but complaining only makes you look bad. Don't do it.

5. *Why would you rely on test results when you can see that I can do the job?* It isn't your job to tell the interviewer

how to make a hiring decision. If assessments are part of the process, take them and do your best.

Tips

- ✓ Prepare for these extra challenges as you would for any interview: with extra attention on the logistics so that you're not thrown into a panic.
- ✓ For video interviews, practice with a camera (web cam or Skype) ahead of time so that you're familiar with the technology and can address any issues that need to be fixed (lighting, your clothes, make-up, and so on).
- ✓ Do everything you can to forget about the technology and focus on the people. Video interviewing really isn't that different from meeting in person.
- ✓ Watch what you eat and how you eat it when meals are part of an interview.
- ✓ Make your travel arrangements as stress-free as possible. If you're like me and can get lost easily, see if a car service or taxi can pick you up and take you to your hotel. It's one less thing to worry about.
- ✓ Don't take responsibility for things you can't control, such as the weather, flight delays or a technical problem that affects a video interview. Show that you aren't upset by these situations and let the interviewer find a solution.
- ✓ Don't be surprised if an assessment is part of the hiring process.
- ✓ Ask for clarification so that you understand how the assessment will be used.
- ✓ Understand that the company using these tools is trying to make the hiring process better—they're making a concerted effort to get past first impressions and hire on a more objective basis. This could be to your advantage.

PART IV

MANAGING EXPECTATIONS

19

TOO MANY COOKS AND UNCLEAR JOB REQUIREMENTS

With interviewing, you may experience getting caught in the middle of a conflict between those doing the hiring and unclear or even contradictory job requirements. Seen most often in panel interviews where the interviewers react to each other in front of the job candidate, one person might say, "There's extensive travel for this job. Are you okay with that?" And before you can respond, someone else says, "I think we can do most of that through video conferencing, so there won't be much travel." You sit there with your mouth open wondering if you should say, "I'm fine either way."

To some extent this is their problem, not yours, but of course you can't be passive, so a ZAP or a question might help them clarify their goals. You could ask, "Is the point of the travel to ensure that our district offices are in compliance?" Notice that sneaky use of the word *our*. Any time you can make it sound as if you're already part of the team (without being presumptuous), you give yourself an edge. Or you can simply take the high ground and tell them that you're open and flexible.

What you can't deal with as easily are nasty surprises such as:

- ✓ a change of location (you thought the job was local and now you have a two-hour commute each way).
- ✓ additional responsibilities for which you may not be qualified.
- ✓ having direct reports or not having them.
- ✓ a total shift in the job description (often to a different function or level).

How can you respond to these wild changes? First of all, see if you can help the interviewers gain clarity about what they need. You have your MAP with you and on the left side you have the detailed job description from the ad, recruiter, or HR. If your interview is more exploratory, then in a way this is easier because your expectations are more open. And by asking questions and listening carefully, you'll find out how your skill set might help this organization.

The kinds of questions you could ask include:

- ✓ What do you see as the greatest challenge facing this department?
- ✓ What do you want to achieve in the next quarter that you haven't been able to in the past?
- ✓ What keeps you up at night?
- ✓ How could someone with my background make a difference in your organization?
- ✓ Are there other people in the company you think I should talk with? (Use this question only when you've hit a dead end—in other words, when it's clear that there is no fit with the department represented by the interviewer.)

Second, do your best to keep an open mind and resist becoming discouraged. I had a marketing client who went on an interview with a leading news organization that was located less than 10 miles from her home. Early in the interview the hiring manager saw her as a better fit for another office that was 50 miles away. My client's impulse was to give up, as she was thinking that this would never work out. But she forced herself to continue to do her best job in the interview and later discovered that this company had a "work anywhere" policy, so although she did have to go to the distant office, she could also work from home as well as in the nearby location.

Remember: Interviewers are busy people with a lot on their minds and they may not entirely know what they need for the position they're filling. Your job is to help them. And you can do that in a number of ways: excellent listening, playback (for example, "If I understand you correctly, your accounting department has been outsourced and you need..."), demonstrating high interest in them (through your non-verbal skills as well as through your questions and your answers), and basically coming across as an enthusiastic problem-solver.

Third, keep in mind that you have a lot to offer, but that you can't be everything to everybody. You will have interviews where you, as well as the people interviewing you, come to the conclusion that this isn't the job for you. Keep the door open as long as you can, so that if there are other areas where you're a better match you'll discover them. But once you know that this is not the case, then the last thing you can do is to use the interview as a networking meeting and find out if there are other resources the interviewer might recommend. This could be other people within the company, people in other organizations, recruiters, professional organizations, LinkedIn groups, and so on. Try never to leave an interview empty handed.

Let's look at a few questions and answers that fall into this confusing category.

Thanks for coming in today, Henry. I think there's been some confusion about this position. We don't want someone in sales, but are focusing more on customer service. (Henry's background is in sales.)

+A. I'm really confused. You have my resume. Why would you ask me in if my background isn't what you need? *Confronting an interviewer is rarely a good idea as it puts him or her on the spot.*

*A. Could you tell me a bit more about what you're looking for? *Much better in tone, here Henry at least stands a chance that he might be able to turn things around.*

!A. I understand that these two areas are different, but in my experience they're very closely related. A good salesperson is an expert in customer service. Can we take a few minutes to review what you need and then determine if my background is a fit? *Starting with a strong sales pitch that negates the difference between these two areas, Henry follows his statement with a ZAP that would be difficult to refuse. He comes across as interested in the company's needs while not admitting that he has the wrong background.*

I know we're looking for a Project Manager, but we were hoping you'd also be able to do some of the programming.

+A. I haven't done programming in years. *Short and blunt, this answer could easily end the interview.*

*A. I started my career in IT as a programmer and I'm a pretty quick study, so I probably could do it. *Still a weak answer, this one is a bit better, but would likely leave the interviewer thinking that this candidate is not a match.*

!A. Could you tell me a bit more about your programming needs? One of my strengths as a Project Manager is that I've kept close to programming. In fact, I was just certified in C# a few months ago. *Here we see an unusual ZAP that is followed by a quick answer. It would be fine to reverse the order too, and give the statement first and then ask the question about their programming needs.*

Extra. (In this answer we'll assume that the candidate doesn't have programming skills.) In my last 10 years at XYZ, I managed complex projects that involved cutting-edge technology. If you talk to any of my reports they will tell you that I understand programming on a deep level and have been able to help them solve coding issues. Can you help me understand what you need the Project Manager to do? *This answer builds a bridge between the two issues of the question: project management and programming, and helps the candidate come across as both capable and confident.*

We've decided to downgrade this position from a VP level to a Director. Do you have a problem with that?

+A. Why are you doing that? Don't you need a VP to run this division? *Sounding annoyed with an interviewer isn't going to make him or her like you.*

*A. Could you help me understand the responsibilities of the revised position? I'm not as concerned about the title as I am the scope of the job. *Using a ZAP and a quick clarifying statement is a good way to deal with this unpleasant surprise.*

!A. I'm interested in any position that allows me to lead a marketing team and make a difference to the bottom line. My goal in my search has been to find a position in which I can make the marketing division of a company highlight the company's strengths and beat out the competition. Could you please tell me more about your thinking behind this change? *With a strong sell followed by a ZAP, this answer keeps the discussion open and positions the candidate as an effective contributor no matter what the title. Not committing to a particular title is an important part of the strategy behind this response.*

What Level Is This Position Anyway?

This example starts with a confession: Grace did not want to network but once she had landed her new job, she told me she understood its importance and knew her search would have been shorter if she'd done it, but she just couldn't get over the hump of feeling that she was imposing on people. Grace was a senior-level operations professional who had been downsized from a high-powered job in the entertainment industry.

She focused most of her energies answering online ads, but when her search had dragged on for almost a year, she got a bit more proactive and went directly to company websites. Finally her phone rang and she had a phone screening for an Operations Director position with a leading consumer products firm. A complicating factor was that the HR screener was from an outside firm (the company had outsourced the HR function), so when Grace asked her questions about the company, she couldn't provide much information. And Grace remembered that this same HR representative had, in fact, called her about a position with another company.

A few weeks later Grace was invited in for a face-to-face interview and had been told that she would be meeting with three people. She didn't know who they were or their titles, or if they'd be meeting all together or one at a time. The only name she had was for the Director of HR (we'll call her Shirley) and Grace told the receptionist that she was here to meet with Shirley. Because she was a bit early, Grace chatted with the receptionist for a few minutes (this helped her feel less nervous) and finally Shirley came to the lobby to bring her back to the conference room. Grace shook her hand and smiled but noticed that Shirley seemed formal and all business. Then Shirley said an odd thing: "I'm taking you to a large conference room, but don't be intimidated. There will just be three of us."

Grace still wasn't sure if this meant all together or one after the other, but followed her into the room and saw that two people were seated on one side of the table. Shirley had Grace sit with her opposite them and the interview began. The two other people said their names, but didn't define their roles (although Grace figured they were the hiring managers) or give Grace their business cards. Grace then surprised them by asking if it was all right if she took notes. (She had noticed that they all had a copy of her resume and a note pad in front of them.) Grace got the strong feeling that they were a bit annoyed by her question because they wanted complete control of the interview. (This, by the way, is a strong sign that you shouldn't use the ZAP technique.)

Grace told me later that it was like being in front of a firing squad—the questions were asked in rapid succession in an impersonal manner. The HR Director took notes and the two others ran the interview. She was asked to walk them through her employment history, why she wanted to work for them, how her previous employees or reports would describe her, how she ran her department, and what she had done on her own to develop her professional skills. A strange thing happened when the atmosphere became more what Grace described as "gotcha." Grace was pretty sure that these two interviewers were on a power trip and she became more relaxed. Maybe that happened because she became less interested in the job, or perhaps because she liked a good challenge and saw this as an opportunity to see if she could turn them around.

At the end, the HR Director told Grace that they had decided to downgrade the job to a Senior Manager role and Grace, once she caught her breath, asked if she could please explain the reason for this change. The answers she got were vague and unconvincing. Grace wondered on her way home if this was a bait and switch situation—if they had intentionally advertised the higher level position to bring in strong candidates, knowing that they were going to hire a manager.

The postscript to this story is a happy one. Grace had received an offer from another company the day before this interview, and had originally thought that she would wait until after this interview to make a decision. But the company had pressured her to decide quickly and because it was a good fit, she had called them on the morning of this interview to accept. That gave her tremendous confidence and helped her cope with the confusion of these unclear and shifting job requirements.

Ditch It!

1. *Why would anyone want to work here? You don't even know what you want!* There are some easy answers that come to mind: it's a good company, the compensation is excellent, it's a place where you could learn and be promoted, and so on. Don't let your frustration with the ups and downs of the hiring process cloud your decision-making.

2. *You didn't tell the recruiter that you wanted someone who can do that.* Although this is true, this statement doesn't help you or move things forward.

3. *Will you pay me a travel allowance if I have to drive 50 miles each way to get to work?* This may be an important point to add to your negotiating list, but during an interview is not the time to start bargaining. It will end the interview quickly.

Tips

✓ Prepare for the unexpected. Try to get yourself in the mind frame that there will be surprises that you'll have to adjust to during an interview and remind yourself that you will not make any hasty decisions.

✓ Stand your ground. When I was asked in an interview if I would help a company with workshops that would have required a daily four-hour commute at a time when I was both moving and working to finish this book, I had to say that I couldn't do it. But I was careful to keep the door open, and the interviewer—who happened to be a really practiced interviewer—understood immediately and put me at ease.

✓ See if you can be part of the solution if there is confusion and disorganization. Ask questions that demonstrate that you are willing to roll up your sleeves and help.

✓ Ultimately, it's not your job to figure out the job description. Do what you can to help, but don't take on the company's responsibilities.

20

WATCH YOUR PRIDE

You may be wondering why there would be a whole chapter on the issue of pride, but as a career coach with 19 years experience, I've seen over and over again how pride can derail a search. Almost all the job seekers I've worked with were let go, although a few "asked for a package" or retired. Having been downsized myself a few times, I understand this issue on a gut level. It hurts to be let go. You feel wounded. You can't figure out why it was you. And in my previous book, *Eliminated! Now What? Finding Your Way from Job-Loss Crisis to Career Resilience*, I go into these feelings in detail and provide case studies to illustrate what my clients did to get past them so that they could be effective in their search campaigns.

Although it's wonderful to feel pride in your work, hurt pride usually creates problems. When you're first let go, hurt pride can get in the way of taking control of your career. Most of us inadvertently give this power to our former companies, assuming that if we're loyal to them, they'll be loyal to us. When this illusion is shattered by being let go, your first job is to reclaim this responsibility.

Hurt and anger tie you to the past, and many clients I've worked with find themselves on a nonstop treadmill on which they replay, over and over again, what happened, who said what, why so and so was promoted and they weren't, and so on.

Hurt pride can also lead you to distort your value one way or another. You could come to the conclusion that if your former company doesn't want you, that no one will. And even as you work on your resume and look carefully at your past work, in this black mood you may decide that you didn't really do anything anyway. This, of course, is a huge de-motivator, making it very difficult to work seriously on finding a new opportunity. At the opposite end of the spectrum, hurt pride may lead you to think that you are indispensable and that without you, your former company will crumble into ruin. Well, that's not too likely either.

Where I see pride getting in the way is in interviews. It takes various shapes but leads to a defensive attitude that gets in the way of good communications. And most interviewers are pretty astute and sense that here is a difficult person—a person with an attitude—a chip on his or her shoulder. Let's look at a few questions and answers that focus on pride.

Can you tell me, Sarah, why I should hire you when your former company just let you go?

+A. I wish I could answer that question! It doesn't make any sense to me after all I did for them. *Here is a person who is clearly hurting and tied to the past. Most of us never really know why we're the ones let go, but Sarah needs to find a way past that and she misses an opportunity here to prove that her value is unchanged.*

*A. I was let go because my company—I should say my former company—acquired its major competition and several positions were cut, including mine. You should hire me because I'm a really good medical writer. *Sarah does a bit better here and gives her exit statement in addition to a rather blunt statement to demonstrate her value.*

!A. What value do I bring to your company as a medical writer and does that have anything to do with what happened with my former employer? (Yes, a magic rephrase.) I'm very excited about this position because it requires my best skills—making complex, medical terminology understandable to a broader audience and ensuring that your clients receive the services they need. If you look at some of the sample publications I've brought in for your review, you'll see specific examples of the quality of my work. Another benefit I bring is that I work quickly. My most recent boss called me "the writing machine" because I can turn out good first drafts in about half the time of the rest of the staff. And lastly, does what happened at my former company have any bearing on why you should hire me? (Rephrase number two.) Absolutely not. If you look at my record at XYZ, you'll see that I was regularly promoted and my references would be happy to tell you about the quality of my work. Would you like to take a look at my portfolio? *This skillful answer uses two rephrases and a ZAP at the end to address the two parts of the question and to mount a strong argument as to why being let go has nothing to do with the quality of Sarah's work.*

Are you trainable? I know you've worked for a long time and I was wondering if you could give an example that shows you've recently been able to learn something new.

+A. Well, I learn all the time. In fact, I like to read computer manuals just to stay up-to-date. *This answer doesn't address the ability to learn that the interviewer has asked about.*

*A. Sure, I think I am. My office door is always open and I'm happy to brainstorm with others when we've got a problem. In fact just a month ago a junior member of my team came up with a really good idea and I backed it. *A bit better, this answer provides an example, but it's weak, because there aren't enough details.*

!A. How have I continued to learn throughout my career? My simple answer to that is through careful listening. When I run a meeting I make sure that everyone gets to talk—not just the outgoing team members. And then I put all our ideas on the whiteboard and work to get consensus from the team. I've also continued to learn by investing in training for myself—whether in management techniques, leadership skills, or technical issues. To give you a specific example, at one of the leadership conferences I attended last year, we learned about the value of gaining 360 feedback. I used that tool to make sure that I was in touch with my team and understood the issues from their perspective. It was really helpful. *By using specific examples and a variety of ideas, this candidate addresses the question behind the question: Are you too old to learn? Or as I like to put it: are you a dinosaur? Using the rephrase technique to create a buffer between the slightly negative question and the answer helps make this an elegant and thorough answer.*

It's been great talking with you, David. Would you have any problem reporting to someone who is about half your age?

+A. No, I'm fine with anyone. *Way too short, this answer doesn't address the interviewer's concerns.*

*A. Not that I know of. I've had a wide range of bosses through-out the course of my career—some were younger and some were older. My trademark is flexibility—I don't really care about a person's age—I'm much more focused on the value they bring to the company. *Here, David uses one of his key attributes—flexibility—to convince the interviewer that he would be fine with a boss of any age. The issue that is left dangling, however, is how he would react to a younger boss who he perceives is not bringing value to the company.*

!A. Would the age of my boss be important? I really don't think so and I'll tell you why. I've learned throughout the course of my career that it's to the benefit of the company to consider diverse opinions. Although age is only one factor, my references would tell you that I'm the kind of manager who works really well with new hires right out of college as well as with senior management. I would assume that I would learn from someone younger, just as I'd hope they might learn from me. *David makes himself an open book with this answer, while being careful not to say that he might have trouble with a younger boss who wasn't interested in his ideas. But he addresses the issue of partnership—of collaborating with his boss—as the factor that would make this reporting structure successful.*

I'm not sure if you know, Beth, but the compensation for this data entry position is a lot less than what you were making. Would you have a problem with that?

+A. I would expect to get paid what I'm worth. *Oh, boy, now we have a huge problem because this answer is defensive and vague. Beth has thrown the "hot potato" back at the interviewer in a non-productive way.*

*A. Could I ask you first what your rate is? *Smart move to use a ZAP to get more information and a bit of thinking time. While still throwing the "hot potato" back at the interviewer, in this answer Beth has done this in an open and non-confrontational manner.*

!A. What kind of compensation would work for me? If it's all right with you, I'd like to table that part of our discussion until later because I'm very interested in this opportunity and am confident we can work out the details. From everything you've shared with me so far, I have exactly what you need—accuracy, speed, attention to detail—and an additional strength—I'm really good at training new hires. Would that be all right? *Of course the interviewer could say "No" at this point and then Beth has got to provide a more direct answer. But in this example, notice how the combination of the rephrase at the beginning and the ZAP at the end create a seamless way for her to deal with the compensation issue. What she is trying to do is lay the groundwork for negotiating reasonable pay.*

Extra. (In these answers, let's assume that the interviewer has said "No" to Beth's ZAP in the previous answer.)

+A. Okay, well I guess I could come down a bit from what I was making. *This answer is like lying down on the floor. Beth has clearly given up.*

*A. I understand that your range for this position is below what I was making previously. Given my experience, can we meet in the middle? *Beth uses a ZAP to see if there is a compromise.*

!A. What I try to do is to consider compensation as part of the whole package. Before agreeing to a specific number, it would be helpful to know about other issues including: benefits, vacation and sick days, and the potential for promotion. I can be flexible if there are good incentives. *Beth has revealed her thinking here and now the interviewer has to decide if he or she wants to make it worthwhile to keep this smart candidate. By broadening the focus beyond salary, Beth has given herself the best chance to score a win-win.*

What Do They Know?

Marty was a database architect with wonderful drive and curiosity. When he started his outplacement program with me after working for one company for 17 years, he was relaxed and always came to his meetings with me in an upbeat mood. As we worked on his resume and marketing plan and also prepared for interviews, he seemed excited about the future. He was a hard worker and had also been helping his parents with their grocery store on evenings and weekends.

Marty's first interview went okay and he had nothing specific to report back to me. But as the weeks turned into months and he didn't hear back from this company and didn't have other interviews scheduled, he began to get discouraged. We talked about the ups and downs of a job search and things he might do to keep himself motivated while also discussing how to run a smart, proactive search.

Finally, he had another interview scheduled and he was prepared and confident. But something happened that threw him: The HR manager was young—really young—and asked him questions that he thought were irrelevant. He struggled to remain positive and to provide good answers to the questions, but he was seething inside. Why did he have to jump through these hoops when the person interviewing him didn't know a fraction of what he knew about data architecture?

In his answers and body language Marty conveyed his deep annoyance. He was not going to play the game and the interview ended on a bad note. And speaking of notes, he wouldn't send the HR manager a thank-you email. As he put it, "What's the point?" As he and I debriefed, I did everything I could to help him over this obstacle, but he just couldn't let go of feeling insulted by being judged by someone so young and inexperienced.

By the time Marty's program ended, he had gone on a few more interviews with the same result, so he decided to put all his efforts into helping his parents with their store, and gave up on finding a way to use his considerable talents in database architecture. His pride got in the way and it didn't allow him to make it past the screening interviews.

Ditch It!

1. *You don't know what you're talking about! Why are you the one interviewing me?* Help! If one of your interviewers doesn't understand what you do, then it's your job to help them get it. This is one of the reasons why, in your preparation, you always work on explanations that will work for those who are in your field as well as those who aren't.

2. *I'd like to talk to the person in charge of the department.* That's understandable, but you won't get there unless

you address the needs of the person interviewing you. Remember, you're the guest.

3. *I was promoted six times in the last four years. Doesn't that tell you I can do the job?* That is certainly a wonderful accomplishment to share in an interview, but don't assume it does the hard work for you. It's your job to listen carefully, ask probing questions, and provide clear and concise answers with a selling point. Nothing else will do.

4. *I was referred in by your CEO. She knows I can do the job, why don't you?* It's fantastic when you get referred to a company through someone in top management, but as in #3, you still have work to do. And again, it's rarely a good idea to confront the interviewer. You might feel good for a minute or two, but you'll lose out on the opportunity.

Tips

✓   It's wonderful to feel proud of your work—you should—but don't let hurt pride get in the way of running a professional and effective job search campaign.

✓   Be respectful of everyone you interact with, whether it's the receptionist, janitor, or CEO. This is a winning quality and will help you stand out.

✓   Get help if your pride is damaging your search. Talk to your priest, rabbi, minister, therapist, EAP counselor (Employee Assistance Act—you're entitled to several free sessions through your former company), doctor, or whomever. Fixing this will help with more than your job search.

✓ Practice answering questions with an open and non-judgmental attitude. This will get you past any hurt pride issues.

✓ Remind yourself of all the things you're good at and of your major accomplishments whenever you feel that hurt creeping back into your thinking. Your employment status may have changed, but your value hasn't. And there are companies out there who would be lucky to have you.

21

BUT I'M SO NERVOUS!

In Chapter 5, as we looked at the power of first impressions, we touched on nervousness. But because this is such a huge issue for so many interviewers, we need to revisit it in detail. Should you be nervous at an interview? Absolutely. But there's a catch. Nervousness isn't your friend and can easily undermine your confidence and cause you to hesitate, not think clearly, and in extreme examples, make it very hard to listen. It can be an all-consuming feeling that makes you shake, causes your palms to sweat, creates a tremor in your voice, makes you speak faster and faster, or causes your eyes to dart around the room. Let's look at some tactics for dealing with this challenge.

You should be nervous because the stakes are high. You need a job and it's not easy to get interviews, so here you are, after all your hard work, and you want the interviewers to like you, to see your competence, and to make you an offer. Another reason to be nervous is that you're facing the unexpected. If I could tell you exactly what would happen, you could be well prepared and more relaxed. But I can't tell you that and neither can any other career coach. You may face an unprepared interviewer, one who is hostile, others who are too busy to give you much time, and still others who really aren't sure what they want.

When I taught presentation skills at Communispond in New York City, we told our classes that nervousness was energy, and that to be effective, a presenter must learn how to channel that energy productively. As I've prepared thousands of job seekers for interviewing, I put it this way: first you need anchors—things that hold you steady and help you through those first, difficult moments. What are they? Solid eye contact and posture (which includes having your feet squarely on the floor and knowing where to put your hands). Then you need ways to burn the nervous energy off through your voice (volume, inflection, pace) and your gestures. In other words, you use up this energy so that it doesn't create a problem or get in the way.

If you are in the lobby of the building waiting for the interviewer to come and get you, sit up straight if you decide to sit down and take some deep breaths. If you need to stretch or do anything else that is more elaborate, do it in the rest room where you won't be seen. If you're standing, keep your posture straight and put your portfolio down on a chair so that your hands are free. Now someone is walking toward you, they say your name, and you look them right in the eyes, smile, walk toward them, and shake their hand. Bravo, you've made it past step one.

Pick up your portfolio and coat (if you're stuck with it) and follow this person, using the guidelines covered in Chapter 6. You make small talk so that this person can get used to your voice and begin to form an impression of who you are. Your physical package, as I like to call it (body, voice, facial expression, clothes, and grooming), is rapidly creating that powerful first impression. So of course you're upbeat, you are thrilled to be there, and are focused on the interviewer. That's the critical part of step two. If nothing else helps you in this chapter but this, remember, when you're nervous, get the attention off yourself and on to them. Find out what they need. Show curiosity and interest.

Step three is the preliminary conversation, a warm up to the real interview (Chapter 7). Sit where you're told to sit, don't lean back in the chair, but position yourself so that you're sitting on the front two-thirds of the chair with good posture, your feet firmly on the floor, and your hands either on the table or desk (but not with your fingers intertwined) or on your lap or the arms of your chair if there isn't a table or desk. Your eyes are on the interviewer—not boring a hole through his or her head, but steady and attentive. If there is more than one person in the room, look at the one who is talking, or if no one is talking yet, at the person who is in charge. You're an athlete ready to compete. You may still feel shaky inside, but don't let that bother you. The interviewer can't see it and once you get going, those feelings will subside. Your mantra is: Get your attention on them. You'll notice that as you do this, that you will have moments where you forget all about yourself.

Step four and you're into the heart of the interview (see Chapter 8 for more on "substance"). You've got your MAP in front of you as well as a copy of your resume, so if you're nervous, you can glance down and pick up a critical thought, the amount of money you saved on a project, or the name of the new system you worked on. (It's amazing what can leave our brains when we're nervous.) Your MAP is another anchor, another way to help you feel confident and focus on what the interviewer needs. Your answers are well organized and logical following the PAR: problem, action, result structure. When you don't understand something, ask a question (ZAP). But if you get the feeling that the interviewer doesn't want you asking questions at this point, stop. Adapt your style to theirs. If the interviewer is a talker, listen. If he or she is quiet and understated, you may tone yourself down a bit, but not to the point where you risk coming across as boring or disinterested. If they have a sense of humor, you laugh. And if their style follows the textbook behavioral interview, you give specific examples that clearly illustrate what you did as well as your thinking process.

Lastly, I believe it's comforting to remember that you will not get an offer from every interview you go on. It just doesn't work like that. If things aren't going your way, do your best to turn things around (probably by using the ZAP technique), but if that doesn't work, remind yourself that this is good practice and perhaps you can still turn this into a productive networking session. (When there's no chance you are going to be selected for a position, you can ask for general advice such as: Are there other areas in the company where my skills might fit better? What recruiters do you use? Are there people outside your organization it would be helpful for me to talk with?) You are always polite, professional, and confident. It's not a great thing to get hired for the "wrong" job. My strong conviction is that you should be excited about your new opportunity. It won't be perfect, you may have to adjust to a long commute or to learning new skills, but it should feel good. If you're under intense financial pressure to find a job now, you may have to park this idea and do your best to make the job you've found work for you until a better fit comes along.

Here are a few examples that illustrate what nervousness can do to you and how to channel that energy so that it's productive. These examples would be better if you could see and hear them, because our body language and voice are almost always what convey nervousness.

Thanks, Alice, for coming in today. Did you have any trouble finding our office? (You should recognize this as an ice-breaker question.)

+A. What? Oh, no. It was fine. *Alice is clearly having trouble concentrating and doesn't use this initial question to her advantage.*

*A. I'm very happy to be here. *While a bit less jittery, Alice isn't answering the question—a clear sign of nervousness.*

!A. No, your directions were perfect and it was an easy drive. *Just long enough to not become a "hot potato," this answer shows confidence and poise.*

Fred, I'm not sure I understand why you were let go from your previous company when you were the star of the sales team.

+A. Well, I don't either, so I don't know what to tell you. *Here, nervousness makes it impossible for Fred to give a convincing answer.*

*A. I thought that, um being a top performer would, you know, like, keep me safe, but it didn't. *Non-words like, "um", "like," and "you know" are another clear sign of nervousness.*

!A. What happened at XYZ that led to the outsourcing of the entire sales team? Let me walk you through the steps that top management took in an effort to cut expenses. (I'll skip the rest of Fred's answer.) *Fred uses the rephrase as well as the next sentence to give a thorough answer while demonstrating that he has nothing to hide.*

Susan, you didn't answer my question. Can you start immediately if we hire you?

+A. No. *This rude answer is likely to cause the interviewer to go from annoyed to ending the interview. Many times these one-word answers come from nervousness.*

*A. I don't know. I have to, well, I need to check my calendar. *Susan is communicating her lack of confidence in this evasive answer.*

!A. I'm sorry, that was my fault. Yes, I'd be happy to start immediately. I may have one or two small things to clear from my calendar, but I'm sure we can come to a mutually agreeable start date. *Always take responsibility for "mistakes" as Susan does here, and follow that with an upbeat response.*

I Really Don't Like to Talk

I thought of that saying "still waters run deep" when I met with Aidan. He was clearly very smart and had been promoted from programmer to project manager. As we worked together on his search, he told me that he was allergic to networking as well as interviewing, and was going to have to find his next opportunity online.

"But Aidan," I had said, "at some point you're going to have to talk."

He nodded.

"An interviewer is going to ask you questions and you'll have to answer, right?"

Again a little nod. Then a confession: "It makes me uncomfortable. I don't like to talk."

I took a deep breath and wondered how I could help him over this obstacle. What I have learned from working with many job seekers with technical backgrounds (IT, science, engineering), is that once they're engaged in a conversation about their area of expertise, the floodgates open and they can talk very eloquently.

Every time we met we practiced answers to a few, typical interview questions. In the beginning he would stare out the window and think for several minutes. After a few weeks, however, he was better and could answer more quickly. Finally, a friend of his introduced him to a recruiter who had a position that was a good fit, and Aidan was now in full panic mode, as he had an interview in less than a week.

We started with the interview MAP, which he agreed was a good tool, and we practiced how he would answer both substance and fit questions. He would be in the middle of an answer and put his head in his hands.

"I can't do this," he told me.

"Yes, you can. Of course you can. Let's back up. When you look at this job description, is there anything here you can't do?"

He shook his head.

"So they'd be lucky to find someone like you, yes?"

"Those are your words," he muttered.

"But they would, so your task is simple. Show them you can do the job."

We also discussed the power of good listening and here Aidan had an advantage that most non-talkers do. I reminded him that listening is a powerful part of interviewing and that in this area he would be fine.

We went back to our practice session. On the day of his interview, I held my breath and waited for his feedback, which he had promised he would send as soon as he got home. Here's what his email said: "Did fine."

When we met a few days later to go over the interview, I was amazed. Aidan had been nervous and extremely uncomfortable, but he had paid attention to the interviewer and had answered his questions well. He had a date to come back in to meet the CIO and the head of HR.

"You did it!" I told him.

He smiled and shook his head.

The second interview went well, too, and Aidan had an offer. It was a fantastic accomplishment because he had pushed through tremendous resistance, and despite his intense dislike of talking, had communicated effectively that he could do the job well and was interested in the challenges of this work.

Ditch It!

1. *I'm not good at explaining what I did. It just worked, that's all.* Like Aidan, you've got to be as effective as you can be in explaining your background. Like it or not, you've got to talk.

2. *I don't understand your question and I'm not sure I can. I'm just so nervous.* Admitting to nervousness is rarely to your advantage. Do your best to work through it. An example of when it might work would be something like: "This is the first interview I've been on in years. I apologize if I seem a bit nervous." This could enlist the sympathy of the interviewer.

3. *I'm going to sit on my hands so that you can't see that they're shaking.* Yes, a client of mine actually said this at an interview. The real damage here is that if you're sitting on your hands you're going to look very strange and you can't gesture and burn off your nervous energy.

Tips

✓ Admit that interviewing is likely to make you nervous and have a clear strategy for dealing with it. This could include your MAP, thorough research on both the company and the people you'll be seeing, good practice so that you're used to explaining your background and accomplishments in a concise and logical way, and knowing how to work through your nervousness (using your voice, posture, eye contact, and gestures). And don't forget your mantra: get the attention off you and on them.

✓ Ask people you know how they dealt with difficult situations like interviewing (performing is way up there on the stress meter). Be specific so that you get a good sense of what pulled them through.

✓   Go to networking/association meetings and introduce yourself to people you don't know. This is a great dress rehearsal for interviews. As you're planning your search schedule for each week, try to set up a coffee date with someone you don't know who might be helpful.

✓   Remember: You're nervous because you care and because finding a new position is so important. You should feel this way, but need to know how to work through the jitters so that you're able to pay attention and concentrate during the interview.

22

OTHER CHALLENGES

There can be other issues that complicate the interviewing process. These could include long-term unemployment, disabilities, not having a reference from your most recent boss, chronic illness, intense home responsibilities such as caring for an elderly parent or a sick child, negative performance reviews, demotions, getting fired, a prison record, and so on. The challenge here is often what to tell a potential employer and when. You want to be honest, but you don't want to be taken off the short list because of one of these issues.

The best place to start is by knowing your rights. Can an employer not hire you because you're pregnant or have a chronic illness? Yes and no. Richard Bolles and Dale Susan Brown have a wonderful book, *Job-Hunting for the So-Called Handicapped* that will give you in-depth answers to these questions (their premise is that all of us either are or will be handicapped in one way or another). As mentioned earlier, The Americans with Disabilities Act (ADA) makes it illegal for employers to discriminate in the hiring process based on disabilities. What Bolles and his coauthor Brown do very nicely in their book is to demonstrate the myths that have been perpetuated by the ADA, while respecting its intent.

A few years ago I was working with a deaf client who had been very successful. As I got to know him (I can get by in American Sign Language so we were able to communicate), I discovered that he was not in any way held back by not being able to hear. He used email and text messaging, at meetings he asked people to write on the white board, and he had educated his management and coworkers about deaf etiquette so that they knew, for example, to face him when they spoke. He was so good at his job that he was regularly promoted, but that, as we all know, didn't stop his job from being cut when the company downsized.

His resume was strong and he started to get responses from recruiters. When they asked to set up phone interviews, he would email them back and explain that because of a hearing problem, he needed to interview in person with an interpreter (and he was willing to pay for this) or through instant messaging. Over and over again, the recruiters either didn't return his emails, or told him that he wasn't the right candidate. Was this discrimination and was it illegal? Yes and yes, but he knew there was little point in taking legal action because it would be expensive, long and drawn out, and might lead nowhere, as the recruiters could simply say that his qualifications didn't match what their client company wanted.

His solution was to look for companies that made products for the deaf, and although this involved relocating his family, he felt it was worth it. In other words, he was finally in a place that provided minor accommodations, where his considerable skills could be used.

The special challenges that we're looking at in this chapter don't change what we've already discussed. You still have to prepare. You still need to know your key strengths and be able to articulate how you can make a difference. And you still have to go through the interview process—whatever that might be. The challenges or special issues are just another layer—another aspect that you should have a strategy for so that they don't create an obstacle.

What about chronic illness? One of my clients had MS (multiple sclerosis) and walked with a cane. He had an extensive background in financial services and had been with his previous company for 20 years. His illness struck during his last five years, but he had remained a strong contributor despite dealing with MS. As he and I worked together, he asked me if he should tell potential employers that he had MS, or wait until he had an offer and was faced with a physical. We decided on the second choice.

I don't know what happened to him because his program ended before he had landed new work, but I believe, from what he had shared with me, that fear about his illness on the part of potential employers was a factor in prolonging his search. As with any search, think about how an employer would see the issues you're dealing with and do your best to address them in an honest way that demonstrates you can do the job. Research shows that one of the great benefits of hiring people with disabilities is they're often highly motivated and more likely to stay on the job.

Another illness example happened to a client of mine this past year. Louise was a PhD and MD scientist with an incredible background in her field. She was not only smart, but she was also charming and unpretentious. Her team loved her and I could see why. After working together for a few months, she told me that she had some bad news that she needed to share with me: she had been diagnosed with thyroid cancer. I put her program on hold while she went through surgery, chemotherapy, and radiation. When I checked in on her every few weeks, she sounded tired but maintained her optimistic attitude. This certainly put her job search in perspective.

When she regained her strength and was about to come back to restart her program, her oncologist discovered that she had stomach cancer and she had to go through a whole new regimen of treatment. Because she lived alone and her family was on the West

Coast, I was concerned about how she would make it through this setback. But she did. She was resilient and believed that not only would she get better, but also that she'd find a satisfying new job. But because of her illness, she couldn't put the time or energy into looking for work.

But then a wonderful thing happened. Just as she was on the mend from the stomach cancer, one of her friends from her former company forwarded an executive job lead to her which was a perfect fit. Louise applied and her friend contacted the head of R&D to put in a good word for her. At almost the same time, she received a call from an executive recruiter who saw the resume she had posted online before her illness, and brought her in for preliminary interviews. The end result was that Louise had two offers—both high-level positions that gave her a promotion from her previous job. She and I evaluated the two and she chose the one that she felt would be most exciting. She then negotiated a later start date so that she could spend a few weeks with her family in California.

What about long-term unemployment as a challenge? How might you explain that to an interviewer? The first part of your answer could be that you aren't looking for "any job" but that, in your search, you've been proactive and are looking for the "right opportunity." Everyone knows that can take longer, so it's an easy way to begin to dispel their fears. Another part of your answer should be to show what you've done to stay up-to-date in your field. If you've gained a new certification, talk about that. If you've taken a course or taught one, that's good too. And lastly, many job seekers whose searches have lasted a year or more find opportunities for some kind of work, whether it's helping a friend who has his or her own business or working in retail. I mentioned in my first book senior managers who delivered newspapers or drove a limousine. You do what you have to do. And lastly, don't discount volunteer work.

The most difficult challenge of long-term unemployment in my opinion is emotional or psychological. After a few years of looking and endless rejections, it's very difficult for most people to believe they will ever work again. ABC's *60 Minutes* ran a wonderful segment in February 2012 about a program in Connecticut called Platform to Employment. This public-private partnership enrolls people whose unemployment benefits have expired in a five-week boot camp to help them face their depression and fear and to prepare them to re-enter the workforce. This is followed by an eight-week internship (paid by this organization), which often leads to a job offer. Take a look at this inspiring story at *http://unemployed-workers.org/sites/unemployedworkers/index.php* and look for resources in your community if you're facing a similar challenge.

But what if you left your former company under a cloud? What if you were fired or received poor performance evaluations or can't use anyone as a reference? Damage control is my answer. Figure out what you can say that is truthful, such as, "When most of our functions were outsourced, I didn't agree with management about how to run the Customer Service Department, and therefore my former boss isn't the best reference. I'd be happy to give you the names and contact information of several customers who can tell you firsthand what kind of service I provided."

You never want to come right out and say you were fired, but you can explain what might have contributed to a difference of opinion or strategy. Most importantly, if you have to have these awkward discussions, come across as calm and confident. We all know that there are two sides to every story and your job is to give yours without showing how angry you are or how your former company betrayed you. Keep those conversations for your dog, who won't mind at all!

What about the age issue facing thousands of Baby Boomers? A recently published *Journal Report* article from October 22, 2012, "Where They Stumble," covers the most common interview mistakes made by the 50 and up crowd (or what I like to call "mature" job seekers.) These include things such as: "inflexibility in work schedule" or the "inability to sell themselves during the interview process." Remember: If you're in this demographic as I am, you have a great deal to offer, but you must show enthusiasm to counter stereotypes about older workers.

When There's a Bun in Your Oven

Ann was five months pregnant and had an interview scheduled in two weeks. "What can I do?" she had asked me. "My clothes don't fit and they're going to know that before long I'll have to take time off. I don't think they're going to hire me." I already knew that this was her second child, so I asked her what she had done when her first baby was born. "I took off six weeks, then went back on a three-day a week schedule, and a month later was back to full time."

"How did that affect your department?" I had asked. (Ann was a biochemist.)

"They were fine. I did a little work from home so that if they needed my help, I was available."

"So," I had continued, "there is your answer."

"You mean tell them what I did the first time?"

"Yes, because your job is to reassure them. They don't want to hire someone who is going to leave, but you can offer them proof of how responsible you were the last time and there is no reason to think this will be any different. Right?"

Ann nodded.

We considered not mentioning her pregnancy, but she and I had agreed that this wasn't the best strategy because her new employer might feel tricked or upset that she hadn't been straightforward with them. She went on the interview, told the hiring manager that she was expecting and when the baby was due, and carefully explained how she had handled her first pregnancy. When she reported back to me, she told me that he seemed fine with it.

She was called back for another round of interviews that included giving a presentation, and after that her references were checked and she had an offer. After negotiating a few minor issues, Ann accepted the offer and worked for the four months until her baby arrived. After her maternity leave, she returned to work and everything was fine. What could have been an obstacle or challenge wasn't, because Ann successfully handled any fears her new employer might have had.

Ditch It!

1. *I really don't want to talk about my health. I'm on medication but it won't affect my ability to work.* By raising an issue but then being secretive about it, this answer creates mistrust. Only after an offer is made can the employer require a medical exam, and then only if it's standard practice. All your medical records are private property and an employer can only see them if you give them permission.

2. *I need a special desk chair because of my size. Will that be a problem for you?* Save accommodations until after you have a written offer, and then submit your list along with a reminder of how excited you are to join the company.

3. *I can't give you any references because I'm not on speaking terms with those idiots at my former company!* Oh, boy, this is going to hurt you. Come up with a safe reason why you can't use references—maybe it's company policy not to give them—or, someone else saw your work in more detail (a supplier or outside contractor).

Tips

- ✓ Know your rights as an employee but be careful not to come across as a litigator.

- ✓ If you're facing one of these or another challenge, create a strategy for explaining your situation that is honest without creating problems for potential employers.

- ✓ Talk to other people whose situation might be similar to yours. There are hundreds of support groups out there and you can be certain that someone in one of those groups has had to explain his or her situation in an interview.

- ✓ Provide proof of why they should hire you. This will overcome many possible obstacles.

- ✓ Tap into resources that can help you, such as the National Federation of the Blind or the National Resume Database for People with Disabilities (NBDC).

- ✓ Don't assume you know what is going to happen in the hiring process. Pitch your skills and abilities effectively. After that, it's out of your hands.

- ✓ Whenever possible, use your network to get inside help. If you have a strong referral, that will go a long way in helping you past any possible problems.

PART V

PUTTING IT ALL TOGETHER

23

CLOSING THE DEAL

Here we are, getting close to the end of the voyage. You know how to prepare for an interview, you're comfortable with the different types of questions you may be asked and know how to answer them, you're acquainted with the different kinds of interviews and understand their purpose, and you know how to manage your expectations. As we've gone through this, you've been exposed to sample questions with "good," "better," and "best" answers. You've also seen case studies that give you specific examples so that you can see the concepts in action. As I like to say to my clients at this stage, "You're armed and dangerous."

What's left? A quick review of interview feedback, how to prepare a wrap-up statement, ways to follow up after your interviews, and negotiating tips. In your toolbox you now have:

- ✓ The interview MAP (and the critical role that research plays in your preparation).
- ✓ Accomplishment stories or PARs (problem, action, result).

    ✓   An additional list of your key strengths and attributes.

    ✓   Ways to practice for interviews including working with a search buddy and attending networking meetings.

    ✓   An understanding of active listening and why it's so important in interviewing.

    ✓   The ZAP technique (so you can find out what employers want).

    ✓   The rephrase tool for turning difficult questions around and managing conflict.

    ✓   Awareness of the power of first impressions and how to use them to your advantage.

    ✓   Specific guidelines for posture, gesture, voice, note taking, and eye contact so that you have a unified and convincing message and can burn off your nervousness.

The two most challenging parts of the interview process are the beginning and the end. Maybe it's a bit like flying a plane with takeoff and landing being fraught with the most pitfalls. The start is hard for most of us because that's when we're most nervous, taking in a lot of information (about the people, building, protocol, and so on) and we haven't had the chance to reduce this nervousness by talking and proving our abilities. At the end, many of us are nervous for different reasons: we don't know how to close and some interviewers aren't particularly good at this either.

Let's look first at what you want to know before you leave:

    ✓   Their next steps and time table.

    ✓   The name and email address of everyone you met with.

    ✓   When it's appropriate for you to follow up (knowing that their planned schedule may slip).

    ✓   How you did and if they have any remaining questions or concerns.

Most of these items are easy to ask for, and again, if you want to be super-polite, ask: May I ask what your next steps are? If you haven't been able to get business cards for the people you've met with, ask the recruiter or the HR representative to please get those to you. After you have an answer regarding their next steps, you could also ask: "Is it all right if I follow up at the end of next week?" This is important because waiting to hear after an interview is difficult and you want to be able to do something to make waiting a bit less painful. And lastly, you don't want the interview to end if you haven't convinced them that you're a good fit, so a final probe to see if they have concerns is a good idea. Here are two samples:

- ✓ "Thank you so much for giving me the opportunity to meet with you and learn more about the XYZ position. Before I leave, are there any areas where you may still have a question about my ability to do this job?"
- ✓ From what you've shared with me, I'm confident that I can do this job and do it well. Do you need any additional information from me?

When one of my clients asked a question like these two, the interviewer told her, "You've only worked for large companies and we're a small firm. I'm not sure you could adjust to much more limited resources." And although this wasn't what she wanted to hear, it was helpful because then she could tell the interviewer that even though she had worked for a large company, her division was quite small, had its own budget and was really run like an independent company. She then went on to ask if controlling expenses was their top concern, and when they said it was, she was able to give a strong accomplishment story that proved her ability to reduce spending.

Now that you've got the information you need, you're standing at the door of the conference room or office where you've been interviewed and it's time to leave. Should you simply say thank you and walk away? As salespeople will tell you, you've got to close or ask for the order. How can you do that in the interview process without coming across as pushy or demanding?

Link thanking the person or people with a strong statement that proves why you're a good match and don't be afraid to say that you'd really like this opportunity. If this feels creepy to you, you're not alone. Practice, find your own language and style, but try not to leave interviews without making it very clear that you want the job. It's a huge compliment to the person and the company if you say that you'd love to work there. And if you're still hesitant, remember, other candidates will do this and then you could be perceived as not really interested in the job.

Elliott's Winning Wrap-Up

Elliott's search went on much longer than he expected. He was let go from a major financial services firm at the end of November, and a year later he was still looking. He was in what I call "almost land"—that is, a final candidate who came very close to getting offers. Although Elliott's program with me had ended, we stayed in touch and he gave me permission to share what he had learned. Here are his words:

"At the end of the interview, I generally close by first stating that I am extremely interested in the position and sometimes bluntly stating that I want the position. This tends to throw the hiring manager off guard. I then ask about next steps.

"When the hiring manager tells me that he or she has: (a) just started the process, (b) is looking at a number of other candidates, or some iteration of this, I directly (with a big smile on my face) ask the hiring manager what it would take to persuade him or her right now that I am the right candidate. This is another way of restating bluntly and directly that I want the position. What I have learned is that most candidates are not this direct and the hiring manager will sit up and take notice.

"The next day, I follow-up with a thank you note which emphasizes just how interested I am in the position."

Elliott didn't start out being this direct, but as he gained confidence from going on interviews, he realized that as long as he wasn't demanding, but rather demonstrated strong interest in joining the company, he was gaining an advantage. Unlike asking, "When do I start?" his closing statements didn't take the power away from the hiring manager, and didn't cross the line from proactive to obnoxious. He left his interviews knowing that he had done everything he could to prove that he was a good match for the position and that he had come across as highly motivated to join the company. It worked. Elliott has now been in his new position with an investment firm for almost a year and is doing very well.

Ditch It

1. *When do I start?* This is an overly aggressive or presumptuous way of asking for the order and takes the decision-making power away from the interviewer.

2. *Why would you hire anyone else?* This is very risky, because an easy response could be "Because they're more qualified than you are."

3. *Can't you see that I can do this job?* The problem here is tone—you sound demanding and irritated, which is not a good combination. If you've done a good job providing proof of your skills, motivation, and value, you shouldn't have to ask this question.

Tips

✓ Make a list of the key things you need to know before you leave an interview. This is a critical part of your preparation.

- ✓ Plan your wrap-up statement, knowing that you'll probably have to adjust it as you'll gain more information during the interview.
- ✓ Ask for business cards. If you can't get them, have the recruiter or HR representative give you the email addresses for everyone you met with.
- ✓ Be creative about additional ways to "sell." You could give the interviewer a copy of your MAP, or provide a list of key competencies and strengths.
- ✓ Prepare ahead of time the answer to this question: "Why should we hire you?" This forms the basic content of your wrap-up statement.
- ✓ Show enthusiasm through your words, body language, and facial expressions. You can't say you're excited and be slumped in your chair. Practice this in your daily conversations.
- ✓ As Elliott did, get comfortable (or less uncomfortable) with saying, "I really want this job." After you've done it once or twice, it won't be that difficult.

24

EVALUATING YOUR INTERVIEW AND PROCESSING FEEDBACK

You're relieved, exhausted, possibly feeling really good or maybe disappointed, but no matter what, the interview is over. You did it. Give yourself a nice pat on the back, because this is really hard work, but as quickly as you can—in the lobby of the building, in your car, on the train—debrief. This is essential, because you want to evaluate your interview and learn from it. And the longer you wait, the harder it will be to remember the details. Because this is just for your own eyes, use any kind of shorthand that makes sense.

I like to start by jotting down three things I did well. My list might look like this:

1. Established good rapport with both interviewers.

2. Listened carefully and asked questions that proved my interest in the position and company.

3. Gave several specific examples that backed up my competitive advantage.

Starting with the positives isn't an accident. It's critical to give yourself credit for what you did well. Then list a few things you wish you had done differently. My example:

1. Moved out of the uncomfortable chair—it was distracting to perch on the front edge.

2. Not said "I love to talk." Where did that come from?

3. Set a date for follow-up with the second interviewer (the hiring manager's assistant).

As I look at my pros and cons, I realize that the things I wish I had done a bit better aren't major—they shouldn't jeopardize my chances. Then I jot down what I've learned about the company:

1. Really nice people

2. Driven by strong value to serve

3. Suspect compensation is low, but this may be offset by other benefits

4. Location not perfect but remote work may be possible

5. Involved in cutting-edge new projects

What should you do now? Look at your notes a few times, and once you're home, treat yourself to some relaxing time, whether that's taking a run or a hot bubble bath. You have used up a huge amount of energy concentrating, dealing with your nerves, and handling the logistics, and now is the time to refill the well. This is why it's best not to schedule two interviews in a day or even one day after the other. If possible, give yourself a break. Tell a few close friends or family members how you did, but don't exhaust yourself by calling everyone you know. That's not a good idea for another reason—you don't want to set expectations too high, because it will be difficult for you if you keep getting calls about "the offer" when either you haven't heard anything yet, or you've been turned down.

You are, of course, going to send a thank-you email to everyone you met with during the interview, and if you took notes on your MAP, you have reminders that will help you tailor each note to each person. For example, let's say that when you met with Will, who would be a colleague, he told you about a new cost-cutting initiative. In your note you will mention it, because it shows you were paying attention and value his information.

But let's say the hiring manager had asked you for an example of a problem you weren't able to solve and your mind had gone blank. At 3 a.m. after the interview the perfect example comes to you. You will now include that in your thank-you email. This is why I don't recommend sending the notes immediately after the interview. Give yourself time to debrief and for these creative ideas to surface. Here's an example:

Dear Molly Sauer:

It was wonderful to meet with you yesterday and to talk with members of your team. I am so impressed by the level of customer service you provide. It's obvious to me that your company lives by its mission statement.

As I thought more about one of the questions you asked me, I realized I didn't give you the best example. At my former company we routinely used customer surveys, but had a difficult time getting customers to fill them out. I organized a committee to look into this challenge and I thought we had come up with some excellent ideas. What I found out later was that our technology (the survey was done online) had several glitches in it that bumped customers off line before they had completed the survey. So although I wasn't able to personally solve the problem, the work that my committee and I did eventually led to a solution.

> *Thank you so much for the opportunity to meet with you and to learn more about the work you do. I'm confident that my skills and experience are a strong match for this position and I look forward to hearing from you. I'll follow up next week.*
>
> *Best Wishes,*
> *Bob Jones*
> *email address*
> *phone number*

What Bob is doing here is fixing a mistake, and this is smart for a few reasons: It shows he's really interested in the job, he demonstrates confidence by admitting that his answer during the interview wasn't the best, and he reminds the hiring manager that he is a good fit for the position.

In other words, your job in your follow-up thank-you notes is to "sell" yourself one more time with the added advantage that you now have met the people you're writing to. Take what you've learned during the interview and turn it into yet one more reason why they should hire you. Of course, if you found out during the interview that this is not the place for you, then you can either politely say so, or simply thank them and see what happens. I suggest keeping the door open as long as possible so that if there are better opportunities within this organization, you'll have a chance of finding out about them.

But what should you do if you made a serious mistake during the interview? What if you had been unable to show that you can do the job or if you became tongue-tied and were unable to speak intelligently? Apologize, explain that you were nervous (perhaps because this was your first interview in years), and show interest in the company. Although this certainly may not put you back in the running, it's the best you can do. Here's an example, using the same people as the previous note:

Dear Molly Sauer:

It was wonderful to meet with you yesterday and to talk with members of your team. I am so impressed by the level of customer service you provide. It's obvious to me that your company lives by its mission statement.

I apologize that I wasn't able to give you good examples of the ways my background fits your needs. This was my first interview in several years, and I'm afraid my nerves got in the way. What I wish I had told you yesterday was that in my role as a customer service rep for XYZ, I learned the difference between adequate customer service and great customer service, and I'm confident I could be an effective part of your team. If you have a chance to talk with my references, they will confirm my commitment to quality.

Thank you very much for the time you spent with me, and I'd be happy to come back for another meeting. I look forward to hearing from you, and will follow up in a few weeks.

Best Wishes,
Bob Jones
email address
phone number

And now what do you do? Move on, fill the pipeline, and let go. As I've said many times, interviewing is a skill that requires practice. Learn from your "mistakes" or the things you wish you had done differently and don't let your search grind to a halt. That will create a huge problem that will delay your getting hired.

Now let's look at feedback. What can you expect to find out when you're turned down after an interview? Here's a sample that a client of mine received recently:

Dear Lucy:

Thank you for your interest in XYZ. After carefully reviewing your application, we are sorry to inform you that we will not be progressing your application any further for the following vacancy: Manager—Customer Service, reference number RUSA-01673.

Please be informed that we will keep your information in our Worldwide database; should you want to prevent this from happening, it is possible to remove it at any time. If you have applied for other vacancies, you will receive a separate response for each of these applications.

Thank you again for your interest in working for XYZ and our best wishes for your future career.

Yours sincerely,

Recruitment Team

When you're turned down, don't expect much. Companies are not going to risk going out on a limb to tell you that you talked too much, or seemed angry or were rude to the receptionist. Every once in a great while you can learn something useful, such as: "you didn't seem that interested in the job" or "your knowledge of a particular system was dated." This may seem like small comfort after all the effort you put into interviewing, but please remember that you've gained interview experience and are one step closer to getting a yes.

But what if you feel that the whole thing was really just a huge waste of time? Learn from it. This might mean not applying for positions with those requirements, making better use of your network, or redefining your goals. There is no substitute for experience, for being in the job market and finding out how your particular background is perceived. Don't beat yourself up because you tried to change industries and it didn't work, or you wanted to get out of management but no one you interviewed with believed it. A critical part of searching smart is to be aware of your strategy and to change it when the job market consistently tells you "no thanks."

Stuck

Jerry was a supply chain logistics professional with one big worry: he didn't have a college degree. While he was working, he didn't think about it because he was busy, was regularly promoted, and knew that he did his job well. But when he was let go after 18 years, he was in a panic. I convinced him that we would look at this issue carefully, but that we had to first get him ready for the job market, and only then would he know if this was going to be a deal-breaker.

As I coached him on how to talk about himself, it was obvious that he had strong leadership, negotiation and problem-solving skills, along with a broad knowledge of Microsoft Office Suite and SAP software. I probed a bit and asked him how he had learned these skills. He said on the job.

"And what did you do if you didn't understand something?" I had asked.

"I looked it up and if that didn't work, I found someone who could explain it to me. I was always one step ahead—always thinking about what I needed to know next to do my job and do it well."

"That's a great answer," I told Jerry. "Make sure to include that in an interview."

At about the three-month mark Jerry had an interview and his excitement was mixed with fear. He was sure that the company would reject him because he didn't have a college degree.

"You can't go to the interview with that mind-set," I had told him. "You'll sabotage the whole deal."

He agreed and we practiced how he would answer any credential questions, and when I met with him again a few days after the interview, he was optimistic. He had met with the hiring manager and she seemed to like his background. He wrote a strong thank-you email and waited. A week went by and then another week and Jerry was now convinced that he would never hear from the company.

He knew that the best advice was to keep his search going, but he couldn't do it. He wanted this job and as he waited, Jerry grew more and more frustrated.

"Why did they bother to interview me," he had asked me, "if they weren't going to hire someone?"

"Hard to say," I had replied. "So many things could have happened: they hired someone internally, they put the job on hold, they're busy with other things and haven't gotten to it yet, they're still interviewing, they've changed the job requirements, and so on."

"That's crazy! Don't you think they owe me a response?"

We had a long talk about this one, because it's understandably frustrating not to hear anything after an interview. Jerry had told me that even being turned down would be better than this limbo. And he was right—it would be. What I told him was that he had to move on. He had emailed, called, and had tried to find an internal contact who could help out. I reminded him that he might still hear from them, but that for now he had to get unstuck so that he wasn't paralyzing his job search campaign.

Two months later he landed a position with a consulting firm where his supply chain logistics background was a perfect fit. The issue of his education never came up, but I told Jerry that if this was something that he believed was going to be in his way, why not look into going back to school? Some companies have tuition reimbursement programs, and in some instances it's possible to gain college credit for work experience. What Jerry learned from his interviews was that he couldn't determine if a missing credential would be a problem, and that the only way to make it through the long weeks of not hearing back from a company after an interview was to keep moving.

Ditch It!

1. *If you're not going to hire me, can't you at least tell me why?* If you were in charge you might be able to ask this, but you're not, I'm not, and we've got to deal with the job market as it currently exists. Keep your frustration to yourself and remember not to jump to conclusions.

2. *I didn't mean to say that I had run that department. But I was part of it.* This kind of mistake is going to get you into trouble, because the interviewer may feel that you weren't truthful. And at that point the interview is over. Give yourself every advantage, be strategic, but you must tell the truth.

3. *I don't know how the interview went. There's really no way to tell.* It's true that it's sometimes very difficult to "read" interviewers, but do your best to at least create a pros and cons list after the interview. What did you notice about the office? How was morale? Could you see yourself working there?

4. *I'm going to be in New York for an interview in the morning. What's wrong with scheduling another one in the afternoon?* Although you may be thinking that this is a clever way to save on your train fare, it's not the best plan, as interviewing is too demanding to pack in two in one day. What you won't be able to avoid,

however, are the all-day interviews, and there your interview MAP will help you.

Tips

- ✓ Read over your notes before your next interview. What do you need to pay attention to?
- ✓ Be fair to yourself. This is a tricky process and often it's difficult to tell how you did, but remember, all of us get better at interviewing with practice.
- ✓ Make your thank you emails as specific as you can to prove that you will "fit" well into this organization. (This is why it's a good idea to take notes on your MAPS.) Some career coaches recommend sending snail mail thank-you notes instead of emails or in addition to them. I don't think this is necessary, because most people expect emails.
- ✓ Don't let the lack of useful interview feedback discourage you. Get together with your career coach or search buddy, and review the pros and cons of your recent interview. And if you feel you were weak in a particular area, have yourself videotaped so that you can watch yourself as you practice answering sample questions.
- ✓ If you don't hear anything for several weeks after an interview, find a reason to reconnect with the company. Look for an interesting article about them or see if someone you know might know someone there.
- ✓ Do your best to keep your pipeline full and maintain momentum. This is tricky, because preparing well for interviews takes time, so it's understandable that your other efforts slow down or stop. Once you're past the interview look for new opportunities. Even if you get an offer in a week, your efforts won't be wasted. It's always good to know who's out there and to strengthen your network.

25

EFFECTIVE FOLLOW-UP (HOW TO SHOW INTEREST WITHOUT BEING A PEST)

This is one of the most tricky issues facing job seekers: When do you follow up and how can you do it without making the interviewers roll their eyes when they see your phone number on their caller ID? Let's back up for a minute to see what you might already know:

- ✓ Some sense of the company's timetable based on when they said they would be making a decision
- ✓ Who is the best person or people to follow up with
- ✓ What the company needs and how you match their requirements
- ✓ If there is a recruiter involved, he or she probably has additional information unless they've never placed someone at this company before
- ✓ Possible obstacles that would delay hiring you, such as a national meeting or key deadline, or staff being out because of travel, vacation, or illness

You do your best to get a sense of the company's agenda and time table at the interview, but things slip. Good intentions may not mean much, so when you're told, "We'll be making a decision by the end of the week," this could really mean "in several weeks." And sometimes it even means "in several months." Here's the good news: it has nothing to do with you. But the bad news is that it's awful to wait not knowing if you have an offer or not. You're suspended in limbo after all the time and energy you put into interviewing well.

What can you do? Use the resources you have available to follow up in a way that won't create a problem. If you're unsure of how often to follow up, ask the HR representative what would be appropriate. But if you can't get any guidelines, here's a general suggestion: Let's say you had your last interview on a Monday and were told that you would hear within a week. On Tuesday you send out your thank-you emails to everyone you met with. To keep yourself from climbing the walls or having a huge spike in blood pressure, turn your focus to something else. Review your job search spreadsheet and/or notebook and see who you haven't talked with in awhile. Find the name of a company that someone suggested to you two months ago that you forgot to research. Post your resume to a new website and send it out to several recruiters. Do not call or send any other emails to the company where you interviewed despite the nagging feeling that they have forgotten all about you.

Somehow you make it through the rest of the week and the weekend, and now it's Monday. Surely they will call you today. But they don't. On Tuesday, send a brief and polite email to the person who is most likely to know the hiring schedule. For example:

> *Hi Larry,*
>
> *It was a real pleasure to meet with you and the others at XYX last week. I believe that Bob had mentioned that you should be making a decision within a week, and I wanted to follow up. I'm very excited about the programmer position and am confident that I have the skills to be an effective part of your IT team.*
>
> *Is there anything else you need from me? I don't believe you have my reference list, so if you'd like me to send it to you, please let me know. If I don't receive any feedback this week, is it all right if I call you next week? Thank you very much for your help.*
>
> *Best, Hilda*

What's smart about this email? Hilda reinforces her interest, her fit, and uses her reference list as an excuse for being in touch. She's not just nagging but is also offering new information, and then she ends by giving herself a plan if the deadly silence continues—she'll call. This is clever because some people are more responsive to one form of communication than another, so busy Larry may be one of those people who returns calls but doesn't keep up with his emails.

The rest of the week drags on and now it's the following week, two weeks since your interview. You call HR, but get voicemail, so what do you say and how can you say it without sounding annoyed? Here's Hilda's script:

> *Hi Larry, this is Hilda Martin at 555-555-5555. It was great to meet with you and the rest of the team two weeks ago. As I mentioned in my email to you, I'm confident that this programmer position is an excellent fit and I'm excited to be part of your IT team. Could you please let me know what the next steps are and when you might be making a decision? That would be a big help. My number is 555-555-5555. And again, this is Hilda Martin. Thanks very much. Goodbye.*

Hilda again was smart—she said her name and her phone number twice—always a good idea in leaving voice mail—and re-affirmed her interest in the position while politely asking for their time table. Unless she has an inside contact at the company or is working with a recruiter, this is all she can do. Inside contacts and recruiters often can find out why the hiring process is being delayed or if the company has hired someone else and didn't bother to tell the other candidates.

Somehow you make it through another week and get at least some of your attention on other companies. Search the internet for articles about the company, their products, and/or the people you met with. Dig deeper, and if you're stuck, ask the reference librarian at your local library to help you. Then send the article or whatever you've found to the hiring manager, reminding him or her that you met several weeks ago and thought that he or she would be interested in seeing this article. This puts you back in that person's mind and that is really all you can do at this point.

Let's say that now a month has passed. Circle back to HR and politely ask if the position is still open. I know you're probably thinking, "How could they be so rude?" or "Why did they inter-view me if they weren't going to fill the position?" and "Couldn't they at least let me know?" And my answer will disappoint you: They're not being rude, just busy. It's impossible to say what is taking them so long, and very few companies communicate with the candidates they've decided not to hire.

Here's what's left for you to cling to: You did a good job at the interview, you sent your thank-you emails, and you followed up in a professional way. Although it's hugely disappointing to be left not knowing, don't be surprised if at some point you hear from them, or if a connection you made during the interview leads you to other opportunities. Your time and effort weren't wasted, and what I hope you take from this is that you're not alone, it's not personal, and that your job is to protect yourself as best you can from disappointment and keep moving.

When "Yes" Means "No"

Kathleen was an accomplished geneticist who was originally from the West Coast. She and her family had moved to New Jersey for her husband's job several years before, and given her credentials and her network within her field, she found a senior-level research position quickly. But then the institute where she worked lost a major grant, and she was in transition again. (Please notice that I never use either "unemployed" or "out of work." Way too negative.) As she and I got to know each other and worked on defining her goals, Kathleen decided that what she really wanted was to return to the West Coast and to work for a biotech company again.

Kathleen was motivated and organized—a winning combination—and before long she was receiving calls from recruiters for exactly the kind of positions she wanted. She prepared carefully for her interviews, and in a few weeks had an offer from a company in California. After minor negotiations, she accepted the offer and began the daunting logistics of getting her family ready to move back to the West Coast. Because she had asked for a delayed start date, she didn't worry at first when she didn't hear back from the company for several weeks. But then, something seemed wrong when the hiring manager wasn't returning her calls or emails.

At first I thought she was worrying over nothing as she had a written offer, but as the weeks dragged on, I agreed with her that something wasn't right. Finally, someone from HR called her to inform her that the offer was withdrawn. She was so shocked that she told them that they must have made a mistake. When the HR representative had repeated that they were not extending her an offer, she had asked why, but there was no explanation. Kathleen had set the wheels in motion to relocate, she had closed down her job search, and now she had nothing.

As she and I worked on this together, I reminded her that her goal had been to work for a biotech company on the West Coast and that she needed to stick to her plan. With her excellent credentials and experience and her strong network, she decided to send out an SOS, sharing with her network what had just happened, and including her list of target companies. Within less than two weeks, she had an interview with one of these companies, and a week after that another offer. Unlike her first experience, this company stayed in touch with her, answered her calls and emails, and made it clear how excited they were to have her as part of their research team. And they were flexible about her start date so that she would have time to move.

This was a happy ending after an awful experience, and although most career counselors would advise keeping your search going until your start date (or until your first paycheck doesn't bounce if you're really skeptical), my feeling is that this is often very hard to do. Fortunately, having an offer rescinded is very rare, so celebrate when you receive an offer and enjoy the time you have before starting your new job. And by following up effectively, you'll find out if there are any problems.

Ditch It!

1. *What is wrong with you people? You said I'd hear back in a week and it's now been a month?* It's very understandable to feel frustrated by the lack of communication that is common after you've interviewed, but you can't express it.

2. *You let me know if you're interested. I'm not going to call you.* It's your job to follow up, so this doesn't work. Professional follow-up is a great way to demonstrate interest and confidence. Why would you miss out on an opportunity to do that?

3. *Why did you waste my time bringing me in for three interviews if you're not going to hire someone?* That is a mystery and a frustrating one at that. And I'd be surprised if you received an answer to this one. My take on it is, companies mean well, they plan to hire and then go through the interview process, but a need may change or there could be a change in management, and the priorities are shifted. It has nothing to do with you, but of course it doesn't feel that way. Remember, each interview gets you closer to an offer, especially if you learn from your experience and fine-tune your skills and search strategy.

Tips

✓ Use your interview follow-up calls and emails to demonstrate your interest in a position, how well you match the company's requirements, and your professionalism.

✓ Ask for advice on how and when to follow up.

✓ Make sure that the tone of all your communications is positive—no one wants to hire someone who is grumpy and demanding.

✓ Look for creative ways to show additional value if you end up waiting weeks or months for a decision after an interview.

✓ Keep your pipeline full, which means don't count on an offer until it's in your hand. Be encouraged by positive feedback, but don't let it lull you into closing down your search.

✓ Don't tell your network that you expect an offer because you had a really great interview. This can come back to haunt you. It's fine to say that your search is going well and that you had a really good interview. Keep things understated until you have good news to share.

✓   If you encounter resistance from a company, see if
    there is a creative compromise. Maybe they can't hire
    you now as an employee, but would be open to you
    joining them on a contract basis.

26

NEGOTIATING AN OFFER

You're almost across the finish line with a written offer in hand (an email offer is just fine as well). Whether this happened quickly or was long and drawn out, it's exciting to have a company tell you you're the one. This is what all your hard work, preparation, the interview, and the follow-up have all been for. But now you have new challenges: Should you accept the offer? What should you negotiate? How should you do it?

Here are some questions that will help you evaluate an offer, and if you have more than one offer, you can create columns so that you can compare your answers:

- ✓ Is this work on target with what you set out to do?
- ✓ Does the compensation allow you to meet your financial needs and how does it compare to your previous salary?
- ✓ Do you like the people you met with?
- ✓ Is there room for promotion and growth?

✓ Would you be excited to get up in the morning and work here?

✓ Does the commute/travel work with your other responsibilities?

Then make a list of the things you're concerned about. Perhaps you used to manage a team but now you won't have any direct reports. Or you were responsible for a region but now have oversight for the whole country. In other words, create a pros and cons list and read through it carefully several times. No job is perfect and it's very rare to get everything you want. What you want is for the positives to outweigh the negatives and unknowns.

Of course, your financial needs are the driver—they play the dominant role in what you will accept and when. Let's say that the company that has made you an offer knows your salary from your last two jobs (from the application process.) What can you do if HR then tells you that the top of their range is about 60 percent of your last salary? How important is your past compensation, and is there any way to convince them to pay you what you were paid before? I think of your past pay as a framework, not an absolute, and unfortunately I've seen many job candidates who couldn't get past feeling insulted by low offers. In such an instance you could say, "I was hoping for something closer to what I was making before, as I'll be bringing my extensive experience in X to your firm. Can you help me here?" Don't agree to anything on the spot so that you have time to see the salary issue in the larger context of the job. You might be earning less but have an easier commute, or the company may invest in training for its employees that will help you get to the next stage in your career.

Because negotiating is difficult for most of us, it's helpful to gain thinking time. When you're unsure about an offer, you could say: "Thanks very much. This is exciting, but I'd like to take a few days to think through this carefully. Is it all right if I call you on Monday?" But if you aren't given any time, then do what is best for you, which in many cases would be to accept the offer verbally, but to add that you will have a few questions and possible issues to negotiate. And then see if you can get a few days to do that.

The odd thing about this phase of your search is now that you have an offer, the roles are a bit reversed. You've been proving that your skills and experience meet the company's needs, but now you're considering if their offer meets yours. Although you're in a position of power—because the company would really like not to have to keep looking—you aren't running the show and therefore must be very careful to create a win-win. This is a tricky time as most of us haven't had many positions to either evaluate or negotiate, and the interview itself never gives us complete information about the job.

Let's break down the typical steps that you might go through in accepting an offer.

1. Preliminary positive signs: a tour of the office or plant, questions about when you could start, a change in their pronouns—instead of saying "The candidate" or "The person in this position," you hear the interviewer change to "You."

2. An offer statement: "We'd like to bring you on board" or "We're excited to make you an offer."

3. Your initial response: "Thank you very much. This is exciting." But don't say "Yes" or "No" or commit to anything.

4. You might ask for the offer in writing—both as a safety net and to buy time.

5. Communicate that you will have questions and find out who is the best person to address them—usually HR or the hiring manager.

6. Salary negotiations: See if you can get the company to name the figure first, and do your homework so that

you have some data to back up your request. If you know that other professionals in your area are earning X, that will help you make negotiations less personal and will give you a reason for asking for X if the company is offering less.

7. Don't get stuck on salary alone, but look at the whole package. Maybe you'll be getting stock options and wonderful health benefits. Take a good look at what those are worth.

8. Once you have more details, make a list of the top two or three things you'd like to negotiate. You'll create problems if your list is too long.

9. You will not lose the offer if you negotiate professionally, and by that I mean keeping the tone positive. You must continue to "sell" your value to the company while asking for some modifications to the offer. Remember: The company expects you do to this.

10. Don't take over the company's side of negotiating. Let's say you were offered $50k and you want $60k. It's not your job to figure out how they're going to pay you the higher amount. Your task is to show confidence and value: "Given my skills and the experience that I bring to this position, as well as what I know about my market value, wouldn't $60k be a fair compensation package?" And then (and this is the hardest part of all), don't say anything else. As I tell my clients, pretend that you're putting a large piece of duct tape over your mouth. Let this now be their problem.

11. At each stage, try to have enough time to think things through carefully. This is too important a decision to rush.

12. Be creative in your negotiations.

13. Read a few books on negotiating—it's an art—and ask people in your network how they've succeeded. (Two suggestions from Career Press are *Hired! How to Use Sales Techniques to Sell Yourself on Interviews* and *Secrets of Power Salary Negotiations*.)

Let's say that the hiring manager calls you, offers you the position, gives you a day or two to think about it, and has told you that the salary is $45k. Then he or she asks if you are okay with that. You might say:

"I know that when I spoke with HR several weeks ago we discussed compensation. But given the scope of this position, I believe that something closer to $50k is more in line with this role" or "I'm very excited about joining XYZ and helping you maintain your world-class customer service. I was looking for compensation in the $50 to 55k range."

And then the hardest part of all: keep quiet. Don't fill the silence. Don't dilute your message.

Now the hiring manager says: "I'm not sure we can do that. Our budget is tight."

You could counter with: "I'm confident that you will see the value I will bring to your company from day one, and believe this is a minor adjustment."

And again, you bite down on a pencil or stick a sock in your mouth so that you don't say anything. Remember they want you. They want the work done and they're not looking forward to continuing the search. And, you will not lose the offer, even if their answer is, "Sorry, we'd really like to pay you more, but we can't."

Before you go to Plan B, you need to try one more time. You might say: "I've looked carefully at what your competitors pay for a similar role and it's in the $50 to 55 range. What's the best you can do?"

And again you hold your breath and wait for the answer. If there is no improvement in salary, then look at your list of the other key things you wanted to negotiate and go to your Plan B. That could include: asking for a sign-on bonus, an early salary review, additional vacation, flexibility in terms of your hours, working from home, stock options, a travel allowance, a company car, an upgrade to your title, paying your professional dues and/or for a certification, tuition reimbursement for you and/or your children, and so on.

Try to create a non-adversarial tone in your negotiations. Your job is to get the best deal you can while understanding that the company has limits. They can't pay you more than your boss. They can't give you privileges that other employees don't receive. Repeat as often as you need to that you're excited about this opportunity and are confident of the value you bring to them. This is a huge motivator—they want to make you happy because you're going to be a strong addition to their workforce. And again, please remember, you will not lose the offer by asking. In my 19 years of coaching thousands of people in transition, I've never seen it happen.

Negotiations From a Compensation Director's Perspective

Tina was my client several years ago and has a wonderful background in HR—specifically in compensation. She worked for large manufacturers as well as a small biotech. When she and I talked recently, I asked her to share with me what she has learned about negotiations from the company perspective. The first thing she told me was: "This is not a science." When I asked for clarification, she gave me an example from the biotech firm where she is currently Compensation Director. "We interviewed a candidate a month ago and the CEO fell in love with him. That changed everything so this individual was likely to get most of what he asked for."

The second point that Tina made was that the negotiations start during the interview process, in obvious ways, such as filling out forms that show your past salary, and in subtle ways such as being asked "What excites you about this job?" Past salary is relevant, but isn't as important as how much the company wants you and needs your skills.

I asked her how being in transition affects negotiations and again her answer shows how subjective this process is. If the candidate has other offers, he or she would have just as much negotiating power as an employed candidate, but if they don't, they're more likely to be offered compensation closer to the advertised amount.

What not to do: Tina said it's a huge turn-off if a job candidate tries to negotiate for things the company doesn't offer, such as stock options or a car. She said this makes the hiring company question whether or not the candidate did his or her homework. Another poor idea is to ask for a higher title when receiving an offer. If you really want to be a director, mention it earlier.

Another useful hint: Tina believes that most companies try to make their first offer their best one. They aren't out to low-ball candidates. Lastly, she advises: Be as direct as you can be. This way you start establishing trust—a winning characteristic.

Ditch It!

1. *You've got to pay me what I'm worth!* What you're worth is subjective, and in negotiating, you'll lose if you're demanding.

2. *I heard that you brought in another person at my level for $10k more. Why aren't you offering me the same salary?* What others are paid in the company isn't really your business. If you do have this kind of information you

might be able to use it in a question, such as: *I don't know if this is accurate, but I heard that you have been paying others at my level quite a bit more. Is there any way to increase my starting salary?*

3. *I'm excited about this position, but with my last company I had a car, a laptop, a Blackberry, and four weeks of vacation. Can you match that?* Asking for too much is a sure way to end negotiations. While you probably won't lose the offer, by being demanding you're starting off with a strike against you.

Tips

✓ In evaluating offers, do your best to look at the big picture.

✓ Be open to surprises in your negotiations such as when a company suggests contract work, a new function or location or additional responsibilities, and give yourself time to digest new information. Our snap judgments aren't usually the best.

✓ Prepare your negotiation strategy and prioritize your "wish list." Be creative in creating a win-win and remember you have the most leverage when an offer has been made.

✓ Train yourself to be comfortable (or less uncomfortable) with silence after you ask a question. This is one of the most difficult parts of negotiating. (Steve Jobs was a master at this and also perfected staring at people without blinking. It helped him get what he wanted.)

✓ Keep your tone positive and remind the person you're negotiating with of the value you bring to their company and how excited you are to join the team.

27

YOU'RE NEVER NOT LOOKING

When everything goes well in an interview it's magical, and feels a bit like falling in love. You're interested in them, they're interested in you, and you get to think in some ways you may never have experienced before. Here's a powerful example from a former client of mine, written in her words:

> Beth and I had worked together in Philadelphia, and had stayed in touch with routine emails and calls after she left for another contracting job. She knew I was casually looking for another position, preferably with a shorter commute. After she'd been with XYZ for about six months, she told her leadership that they needed to talk to her friend (me.) As Beth told me "You'd be a great fit, and I'm really talking you up!" she also spent a fair amount of time telling her recruiter, Jim, about me. Finally, XYZ had a couple of projects in the short-term pipeline, and they called Jim, who called me.
>
> I was a bit reluctant—I already had a full-time job and this would be contracting. But a few things swayed me: the hourly

rate, one hour less commute each way, and a clause in the contract with right-to-hire. Trusting Beth, I agreed that Jim could present my resume. (I was apparently candidate #1 in a pool of 1.) After a few calls, the interview was set for 2/8.

The day before the interview, I got a panicked call from Jim. XYZ was concerned about the snow storm predicted for the next day, and they wanted to talk to me in person. Was there any way I could come in for the interview that afternoon? I hesitated. "Jim, I'm in Philadelphia. I've got a meeting that ends at 1:30. And I'm wearing jeans." "That's okay," Jim said. "Jim, I'm not ready for the interview." "That's okay." I finally agreed to meet him at XYZ at 4 o'clock. He said he'd bring copies of my resume.

When I arrived, he handed me the resumes, and we went into the building, signed in, and met one of the directors who would be part of the interview team. Once in the conference room, I met Beth's director and two other managers. I had already decided that I would ignore the "elephant in the room," and didn't mention or apologize for my wardrobe. I operated under the decision that they knew I'd be casual, so what was the point in mentioning it? I figured they wanted to talk to me, not my clothes.

I don't know if it was a result of knowing that I already had Beth's endorsement, or the comfort of not being dressed up in an interview suit, but it was the easiest interview I've ever had, and they got to see "the real me." When they asked me, "What do you do when someone doesn't give you status information?" I answered: "Well, I assume that here at XYZ, as with my current employer, tasers are illegal, so I become more proactive in getting the reports. More stopping by, more reminder emails, more annoying—and sending the message 'if you give this info to me when I first ask for it, I'll go away and leave you alone to get the real work done." Everyone chuckled.

On Monday, Jim called to say "they loved you, but the project list changed. You'll have the next opening, but I don't know exactly when that will be." Jim called three days later and said that I had the job. I waited until there was a signed contract between all parties (2/20), and gave notice to my current employer. I started at XYZ on 3/4.

The moral: If Beth and I hadn't stayed connected, I wouldn't have this great position. And my last advice: 1. Always carry a nice portfolio/pad, resumes, and a good pen in your car. 2. If you've got something actively working, consider putting some "interview" clothes in your trunk. 3. Don't wait until the night before the interview to review your notes. 4. Although it worked for me, you probably don't want to mention tasers during the interview!

Looking for work is rarely a straight line. It's a zigzag, up-and-down process, filled with surprises. Some of these are unpleasant, and others are uplifting, as you've seen in many of the case studies. But no matter what happens, you now have the tools to deal with these ups and downs. You have clear goals for your search and you know how to prepare for an interview and how to do your best in the interview itself. You've read many sample questions and have looked at answers that include an analysis of what makes the best ones. You have a strategy for dealing with the surprises, whether you decide to ZAP or to rephrase a question. And you know how to show that you're actively listening and how to demonstrate that winning quality: enthusiasm.

You're a complete package and your body language supports your critical message about yourself. Although this doesn't mean that you won't encounter surprises, please remember that by looking at the many types of interviews and interview questions, you're ready. And hopefully you've signed on to the concept that "you're never not looking." This means you're managing your career, investing in your future while doing an excellent job in whatever work you do.

Go out there and let people see all the ways you can contribute. Be confident but also be a beginner—that's a winning quality too. And know that as you interview and get better at it, you will get an offer—maybe even more than one. You have *The Essential Job Interview Handbook* to guide you.

I wish you all the best. Please visit my website for weekly blogs, additional chapters (see the QR code on the back cover), and if you have comments or questions go to *www.JeanBaur.com*.

Final Tips

✓ Invest in your career. Whether you're anxious to climb the corporate ladder, or work part-time and do other things, it's your job to keep your resume up-to-date, cultivate your network, and be prepared for interviews.

✓ Don't shut down your search until you're 100 percent certain that your offer is solid. And even then, you're never not looking.

✓ Make interviewing part of your life. After all, it boils down to listening carefully to find out what others want and then demonstrating how you might be able to help. There are many opportunities to do this: at work, for a community project or volunteer work, or at a formal interview.

✓ Develop your own interview style but be sensitive to the culture of the organization where you're interviewing.

✓ Take good care of your references. They're a critical part of this process, and when you land, show your appreciation through a small gift or by taking them out to lunch.

✓ Prepare for the unexpected and remember my mantra: "They'd be lucky to have you."

✓ And lastly, practice, practice, and practice. You don't need to be perfect, you just need to be able to control your nervousness so that you can do your best job and help the company see that you'd be a wonderful addition to their team!

INDEX

ABOUT THE AUTHOR

Jean Baur, career coach and author, has worked in the out-placement industry for the past 19 years. She currently lives in New England where she continues her work with Lee Hecht Harrison, a talent solutions company, as well as teaching her own highly successful workshop: "Boomers Back to Work!" As an independent consultant, Jean knows a great deal about interviewing, both firsthand and in preparing thousands of job seekers for this critical part of getting hired.